James Roche

Appomattox : the war

James Roche

Appomattox : the war

ISBN/EAN: 9783337118983

Printed in Europe, USA, Canada, Australia, Japan

Cover: Foto ©ninafisch / pixelio.de

More available books at **www.hansebooks.com**

The War of "the Blue" and "the Gray."

A THRILLING AND ENTERTAINING DRAMA

IN

FIVE ACTS.

By JAMES L. ROCHE.

MEMPHIS, TENNESSEE.

ERRATA.

At page 28, read immediately after the sixth line:—

Blanche. [With a gesture of astonishment—in pouting tone]
You're taking it very easy, Father—and a "Robber"—
[Looking Rear—in tone of alarm] perhaps a *Murderer!*—
hiding in the House!—

APPOMATTOX.

The War of "the Blue" and "the Gray."

ACT I.

Scene I. [Oldham, a New England Village. Archibald Ferguson's House. An Ante-room.]

Gus Ferguson. [A young New England Lawyer. Tall, athletic, and of erect stature, with a serious, intellectual face. In every-day plain clothes, and wearing a dark soft Hat. With a firm deliberate step, entering by Right Entrance, a package of Mail matter in one hand, and an open Letter in the other. Halting—in soliloquy —in confident serious tone] It has come at last—the evil day on which our Country is to be drenched with fratricidal blood!—on which, from the Lakes to the Gulf and from Ocean to Ocean, will be kindled on our peaceful hill-sides, the Camp-fires of the greatest of "Civil Wars!"—[In regretful tone]—on which it will be the duty of the Northern patriot to go forth to slay his Southern brother!—[Suddenly assuming a gesture of horror—in thrilling patriotic tone] But did the pa· triot Heroes of the "Revolution" fight in vain for American Liberty!—and did they bequeath to their Sons, to be capriciously "dissolved" by them, the sacred heritage of a "Union" cemented with their life-blood!— [In emphatic indignant tone] No!—[Advancing, a step, and vigorously stamping the floor—in thunder tone] a thousand times, No!—[Reading from the Letter in his hand] While we can count them by the thousand yet—the admirers of the "Old Flag"—I greatly fear that the firm friendships contracted at Old

"Stafford," between the "Yankee Boys" and their Southern fellow-students, will soon be ended—that the strong
bonds that made them brothers, will soon be severed—
severed by them in a long impending Conflict!—But
should it be the decision of our State, to raise the Standard of "Secession, and draw her sword in the Cause of
"Southern Independence," that service would be the
most congenial to me, in which—on the "March," and
in the "Bivouac," and the "Battle"—the comrade at my
side should be of my kindred, or of the companions of
my youth; and I should therefore don the "Rebel" uniform [Petulantly laying down the Letter—in rebuking tone]   The hot-headed young Southron!—to a Cause
that at heart he condemns, he would give his sword—and
his life-blood, too—for the poor reason that it would be
the Cause—[In tone of condemnation] the Treason-Cause
of *his* "section" of his country! [Facing the audience—in
confident tone]   But older heads will soon be seen, for
like reason abjuring their allegiance to their Country!—
Indeed, they can already be seen at the Capital of the Nation, in Southern men traitoriously vacating their places
on the floor of Congress!   And they can be seen in the
high Army and Navy Officers of Southern birth, who
are basely deserting their country's Flag, to draw their
swords under the Standard of a Rebel "Section!" And
should further proof be wanted, that abler thinkers
than those Southern students who suddenly severed
their connection with Stafford College, have been de-
luded by the heresy of Secession, we have it in the with-
drawal from the Federal Benches—to go and take up
arms against their Country—of grave Judges of Southern birth! [In startling rebuking tone]   But let them
all go!—The defection of Southern men—that deprives
us of some of our best "Captains"—can only serve to
prolong a Conflict [In vehement tone] that must be
closed—[In solemn prophetic tone] that will be closed
with a crowning victory for our arms!—[With firm step
and erect bearing, he departs by Left Entrance.]

[End of Scene I.]

SCENE II. [Oldham. Archibald Ferguson's House. A large
Parlor. At Middle Rear, and Left, Front of Middle,
wide open Doors. At Middle Left, and facing Rear, a
Writing Desk. At Middle Right, a Mantle-Piece, with
a hearth in which a bright Coal Fire shows in a Grate.
A Sofa against the wall, Left, Front of open Door.
Left of Centre, near Front, two Chairs—the one next
to Left side, a large Easy Chair.]

[Seated at Writing Desk, Miss Bessie Ferguson.
Occupying a capacious Chair, Right, well toward Front,
Ben Adamson, Editor of the "Northern Light;" stand-
ing before the Mantle-Piece, with his back to the Fire,
Blake Stansbury, the Village Schoolmaster.]

[A startling outburst of exclamations comes from Off,
Right Rear.]

Blake Stansbury. [Tall, lank, and conceited—well into the
"Forties"—looking significantly at the great Editor—
in. confident tone] That's late "News" about the
movements of the "Fire-Eaters!"—[With bounding step,
he departs, Right Rear.]

Ben Adamson. [Of robust frame—with repulsive features,
and a bushy head of slightly silvered Hair—well into
the "Forties"—bounding to his feet, and looking Right
Rear—in sarcastic confident tone] The Traitors are
already at their bloody work!—but I've been looking
for it.—[With hasty step, starting Right Rear] Yes—
I've been looking for it.

[The firing of a Cannon comes from Off, Middle Rear]

Gus Ferguson. [With hasty step entering through open Door,
Left, and with a gesture of Horror looking Middle
Rear—in tone of indignation] Have they committed
the fatal overt act—"fired" at the "Flag!"—[Looking
Right Rear—in confident tone] And do I hear the exclamations of indignation that in our quiet village greet
its announcement, as the terrible "News" is flashed
through the land!—[Facing the audience—in tone of
indignation] I am no "Anti-Slavery" Fanatic.—I am
no rampant assailant of the South or her "Institutions."

But when I see Southern men hastily returning from every point of the Compass, to their old homes, and arming themselves for the avowed purpose of forcibly extending the area of "African Slavery" in this fair land, [In emphatic tone] I will henceforth be "Anti-Slavery"—and *Anti* everything—and everybody—favorable to that unholy revolutionary project!

Bessie Ferguson. [A pleasant-faced young lady, well above the average height—of lithe symmetrical figure—a year or two out of her "Teens"—bareheaded, with a wealth of glossy dark Hair in a coil at the back of a shapely small head. Wearing a becoming indoor Dress. Rising and going up to her Brother—in tone of solicitude] Brother, can't they settle it, without going to War"—

Gus Ferguson. [Looking gravely down at her] No—no—my Sister!—[In emphatic confident tone] And "African Slavery" is a blot on the escutcheon of our country, that nothing can wipe out, but the blood of Freemen!—

Bessie Ferguson. [In condemnatory tone] It would be a sad spectacle, Brother, that that would exhibit the brave Men of the North engaged in bloody Battle with their brave Brothers of the South!—[In tone of solicitude] And I hope that my dear Brother will not have occasion to participate in a conflict in which the foe before him should be his Countryman!—may, perhaps, be his Kinsman!—

Gus Ferguson. [In grave tone] What you say, my good Sister, is too true!—[In solemn assuring tone] But my Country needs my sword!—And for a soldier's exciting life, I must exchange the more congenial one of peaceful pursuits—[In sarcastic tone] to fight the battle that Ben Adamson—and Blake Stansbury—and people of their type of thinking have forced upon us!—[Looking gravely at her] And you, too, my Sister, can take part in the terrible Conflict—and help your Country in her darkest hour!—in ministering to the needs of the wounded and the sick.—[With manly bearing and firm step, he departs through Middle Rear.]

Bessie Ferguson. [Looking after him] I am proud of my Brother!—His "War" sentiments are tempered with moderation. He is no blusterer.—He is brave and patriotic, and he will give a good account of himself under his Coun.ry's "Flag"—if we have "War."—

Ben Adamson. [Bounding in, Right Rear –in exultant tone] They've put their foot in it, at last!—[Hastily crossing the Stage] The Traitors have put their foot in it, at last!—[He bounds out, Left Rear]

Bessie Ferguson. [Looking after him—in sarcastic tone] Gone mad at last, on the "Slavery Question"—

Blake Stansbury. [Bounding in, Right Rear—joyfully gesticulating] Glorious "News!"—Glorious "News!"—

Bessie Ferguson. [Approaching him, a step—in eager tone] What is it all about, Mr. Stansbury! —

Blake Stansbury. [He franticly bounds out, Left Rear]

Bessie Ferguson. [Facing audience –in sarcastic tone] There goes another "Radical" Fanatic—with his head turned at last, by his "Anti-Slavery" "Hobby."—[Pointing to open Door, Left—in tone of satisfaction] I'll go on the Gallery—and there I may be able to learn something about this exciting "News"—that is driving the "Radicals" wild with joy—and that threatens to turn our staid old town into a very Bedlam.

Ben Adamson. [Bounding in through Middle Rear—in indignant tone] The "Nullifiers" have put their foot in it, at last!—[In soliloquy—in sarcastic tone] They are seizing the Government Arms and military Stores!—all of them that they had not already stolen!"—and are secretly organizing an Army with which to occupy in force, the approaches to the National Capital—and prevent the "Inauguration" of our President!—[Bounding Right Rear—looking back—in exultant tone] "Forewarned" is "Forearmed!"—

[A Fife and Drum Band playing a lively National air, is heard approaching, Off, Left Rear.]

Blake Stansbury. [Through Middle Rear, bounding in, joyfully gesticulating—suddenly turning round, and pointing Left Rear—in exultant tone] The "Wide Awakes" are coming in!

[Immediately, the "Firing" of Cannon comes from Off, Middle Rear.]

Blake Stansbury. [Joyfully gesticulating, he bounds out, Right Rear]

[The Fife and Drum Band approaching, suddenly stops playing, and from Men approaching, Left Rear— "Marching" to the tap of the Drum—comes, in Solo—in thrilling tone]

We're coming, Uncle Abraham!—
We're coming, all night long.—

[Men wearing high Hats and Glazed Capes, and carrying long white Poles surmounted with small Tin Lamps, with military step show filing past—from Left to Right—at Middle Rear—singing, in solo—in thrilling tone]

We started out, a pitiful few—
But we're now Ten Thousand Strong!—

[By all—in Chorus]

Ten thousand Yeomen from the Hills—
Ten thousand Volunteers—
The Vanguard of the Nation's Hope—
Her Sturdy Mountaineers!

[Suddenly halting and facing Front—in Solo]

We are the sons of patriot sires,
And Patriots, too, are we.—
We march as marched our brave sires, too—
To Death or Victory!—

[By all—in Chorus]

Ten thonsand Yeomen from the Hills—
Ten thousand Volunteers—
The Vanguard of the Nation's Hope—
Her Sturdy Mountaineers!

We tear ourselves from weeping wives!—
From Mothers, too, who'll mourn
And look for gallant "Soldier Boys"
Who will never home return!—
[Raising to their eyes, their Pocket Handkerchiefs—
          by all—in Chorus]
     Ten thousand Yeomen from the Hills—
     Ten thousand Volunteers—
     The Vanguard of the Nation's Hope—
     Her Sturdy Mountaineers!

[Facing Right, and "marking time,"—by all—in
     Chorus]
We're coming, Uncle Abraham!—
We're coming, all night long.—
We started out, a pitiful few—
But we're now Ten Thousand Strong!—
     Ten thousand Yeomen from the Hills—
     Ten thousand Volunteers—
     The Vanguard of the Nation's Hope—
     Her Sturdy Mountaineers!
          [With quick step, they promptly proceed, Right]
                              [End of Scene II]

SCENE III. [Entrance to Encampment of "Oldham Blues,"
     Off, Right Front. A Field Tent—above which the "Stars
     and Stripes" is waving—is in plain view]

Captain Ferguson.)
Ben Adamson.   } [With deliberate step, they enter to-
          gether, from the Camp]

Ben Adamson. [Bounding before the Captain—in savage tone]
     We must not show any mercy to them, Captain!—and
     it will not take us the half of "Three Months," to drive
     the "Traitors" into the Gulf!—all of them that'll get
     away from us in the first Battle!—

Captain Ferguson. [Gus Ferguson, in a Captain's Army Blue
     Uniform—looking composedly at him] How should we
     dispose of the Prisoners whom we should take in
     Battle—

Ben Adamson. [In bloodthirsty tone] Raise the "Black Flag,"
Captain! —and give the "Traitors" no "Quarter!"—and
you'll have no "Prisoners" to "Feed!"—or to ·"Guard!"—

Captain Ferguson. Should some of our misguided Countrymen
lay down their arms, and surrender to us, what should
we do with them—

Ben Adamson. [Violently motioning his arm toward Door—
in emphatic merciless tone] Take the "Traitors" out,
at once—-and shoot down the "Privates!"—and "string
up" the "Officers!"—That's the way t) make short
work of the "Slaveholders'" Rebellion!

Captain Ferguson. What should we do with the non-combat-
ants whom we should meet on our way, in our advance
through the enemy's territory—the old men, for in-
stance?—and the women and children?—

Ben Adamson. [Pointing back—in merciless tone] Dont leave
a living enemy—of either sex, or of any condition—
behind you, Captain!—if you have to burn "Rebel Sym-
pathizers" out of House and Home!—and to drive them
before you, to the Sea!

Captain Ferguson. [In sarcastic rebuking tone] Would you
have a great Army fighting victoriously for universal
freedom, descend from its high plane, to wage upon
defenceless women, and upon the aged and feeble, a
ruthless War of "Extermination!"

Ben Adamson. [Brandishing at him his raised finger] The
pretty enemy in "Petticoats," Captain, has ever been
the Soldier's most dangerous enemy. And should one
of those "Down South" famed "Creole Beauties"—who
are sure to be in great number in the Secret Service of
the Rebel Government, and who, very likely, will be
arrayed in the humble garb of meek "Sisters of Char-
ity"—want to cross your lines, put her down for a
"Rebel Spy!"—[In bloodthirsty tone] and have her
immediately seized, and unceremoniously hanged from
the nearest Tree!

Captain Ferguson. [With affected seriousness looking at
him] Mr. Adamson! what part do you intend to take

in the work of "whipping" those refractory people whose annihilation you so urgently advocate?

Ben Adamson. [Assuming a pompous attitude] Some of us should stay at home, Captain—to run the Government—and to "stir up" the "Boys," when there's a new "Call" for Troops—

Captain Ferguson [Turning away—looking contemptuously back] To do the "Outrage" business, eh!

[An "Assembly" call comes from the Camp, Off, Right Front]

["Blue Coat" Privates run in,' from Left Entrance, and hastily crossing the Stage, bound Right, into Camp]

Ben Adamson. [Pompously approaching him—in blustering tone] And we'll go down there, ourselves, Captain—Blake and myself—

Captain Ferguson. [Starting toward Camp—looking back—in rebuking tone] Yes—when the fighting is all done—and the plundering begins!—

Ben Adamson. [Following him—in arrogant tone] And the New Government will need a little Army of "Loyal" Citizens—like myself—for "Tax-Collectors"—and—

Captain Ferguson. [He motions him back]

Ben Adamson. [Turning left around, and going Front—in tone of ridicule] What "part" do "I intend" to "take" in the great Yankee War of Negro "Emancipation?"—[In sonorous hearty tone] ha! ha!! ha!!!—

Captain Ferguson. [He shows hastily returning. He suddenly halts]

Ben Adamson. [Thrusting his hands into a pair of deep breeches Pockets, and throwing his legs wide apart—in emphatic serious tone] To fill these little Pockets—[Patting his ill-developed abdomen] and to greatly increase this *avoirdupois*—[Putting his hand back down into his deep Pocket, and throwing forward his abdomen—in mocking tone] this is the very "part" that this bold patriot intends to "take" in that bloody Drama—[In sonorous hilarious tone] ha! ha!! ha!!!—

[Glancing right round back—with a gesture of Horror
—in tone of mortification—Aside] The Devil!—[With
a bearing of humiliation departing hastily, Left, looking right around at audience—thrusting his hands deep
into his breeches Pockets, and throwing forward his
abdomen—in undertone—in hilarious tone] "Running
the Government"—and "stirring up the Boys"- ha! ha!—

Captain Ferguson. [Advancing, and looking at audience—in
sarcastic tone] Should he ever follow us, I thought it
would be far behind--carrying an empty Satchel.—
[With hasty step, he departs, Left.]

                              [End of Scene III.]

Scene IV.   [Scene II, repeated]
     [Beside Writing Desk—in view of audience—a large
          Black Satchel sets on the Floor]
Captain Ferguson.)
Bessie Ferguson. }   [With slow step, they enter together,
     through open Door, Left, and turn Front]

Captain Ferguson. [Looking down at her, on his left—in
serious tone] If it depended on my will, my Sister, I
should be spared the sharp pang [Pointing to his heart]
that I feel at this moment--at the thought of my sepa-
ration—it may be for years--from one so dear to me!—
But at Washington, they are looking for trouble,
soon—from some contemplated bold operation of the
"Rebels"—of which they have secret advice.—And
they have called upon the "Loyal" North, for Troops,
with all possible haste!

Bessie Ferguson. [In a Dress different from that worn by
her when last seen, in Scene II--through her tears
looking up at him—in sorrowful tone] Then, that
expectation of the "Politicians" is not yours, Brother—
that on sight of the "Boys in Blue" in force, the Rebels
will throw down their arms, and run back to their
homes; and that, therefore, your mission to the
National Capital will prove a splendid "Pleasure
Excursion."—

Captain Ferguson. [In sarcastic tone] The unprincipled
Politicians!—of both sides!—who are solely responsible
for the impending Conflict, have no idea of the magni-
tude of their joint wicked work!—[In assuring tone]
The brave Men of the South are not drawing their
swords in a Cause that is dear to them, to sheathe them
without "fighting" for that Cause!--[In earnest confident tone] And "fight" for it they will—and "fight"
well!—as they have always done!—done everywhere!—
[In serious tone] And the "Oldham Blues" will be
among the first Troops who will give them Battle!—

Bessie Ferguson. [Looking up at him—in tremulous tone]
How can I tell my poor Father--who is forever asking
for you—that you will leave home, soon!—

Captain Ferguson. [With a gesture of Horror] That in-
formation I want withheld from him—until the last
moment!—[In solemn tone] And would to Heaven
that I could be spared altogether, the torture of a final
"Leave-Taking" with him!

[A Bugle call comes from Off, Right Rear]

Captain Ferguson. [Pointing to open Door, Left—in urgent
tone] Go tell him that I was in the House—asking for
him—[With hasty step, he departs, Right Rear]

Bessie Ferguson. [Looking admiringly after him] I shall
soon lose the best of Brothers!--[Going toward Writing Desk] What more tokens of sisterly devotion can
I give him!--dear momentoes of home—that would be
doubly dear to him when far away!—[Seating herself
at Desk, and pulling open a little Drawer, at top—and
withdrawing from it, a small dark Case, and holding it
up—in sorrowful tone] When he opens this, [Opening
it] he will find what I know he will prize dearly—
[Holding up its contents] a Locket containing his only
Sister's Likeness—and a Lock of her Hair!--[Consigning
the articles to the Satchel, and pulling open, another
Drawer, and looking into it] And when he unpacks
his Satchel, he will find in it—from his dear Father--
what he committed to my charge. to put in his "Dear

Boy's" Trunk, when he would be "going to the War"—
[Holding them up, and tenderly consigning them to the
Satchel] a Meerchaum Pipe—a Tobacco Pouch [Smel-
ling it] filled with the best of Tobacco—and [Fondly
kissing it, as she withdraws it] his own dear Likeness!—
[Longingly gazing at the dear picture—in tone of
sorrow] My poor old Father! [Sobbing, she tenderly
consigns to the Satchel, the dear Souvenir]

Archibald Ferguson. [Off, open Door, Left, halting in a fit of
hard coughing, he is heard approaching]

Bessie Ferguson. [Hastily closing Satchel, and setting it back
out of sight] I dont want him to know what I've been
doing!—[Rising and applying her Pocket Handkerchief
to her eyes] And with telltale wet eyes I dont want to
meet him.

Archibald Ferguson. [Of robust frame, and with prepossessing, venerable features, and flowing White hair—in
loose Dressing-Gown, and leaning on a strong Walking-
staff, suddenly appearing at open Door, Left, he coughs
convulsively]

Bessie Ferguson. [Bounding toward him] My dear Father!—
[Taking firm hold of his left arm, and leading him toward the Easy Chair] You have not yet got rid of that
distressing Cough—

Archibald Ferguson. [Falling heavily into the Chair—in
sonorous despairing tone] No—my Child—and I fear I
never will--get rid of that Cough.—

Bessie Ferguson. [Seating herself beside him, and affection-
ately smoothing back his disheveled Hair—in cheering tone] But you coughed much harder, yesterday,
Father—and you are looking much better, today—

Archibald Ferguson. [Looking around the apartment] I
coul l see my "Dear Boy," every day—before they
made him "Captain" of the "Company."--[In tone of
satisfaction] But may be he hasn't the time to spare—
from his important duties.--And I want "Gus" to be a
good Soldier -- and a Patriot—like his Father.--[In tremulous tone] He's all I have!--but I'm willing to give

him to my Country—in her present hour of great peril!—

Bessie Ferguson. [Sobbing, she turns her face away]

[A thrilling martial air comes from Off, Right Rear]

Archibald Ferguson. [Glancing Rear—in soliloquy—in grave tone] I always believed that it would come to this— soon or late!—But I didn't want to live to see it!— [Abstractedly—in tremulous tone] We'll be very lonely, when "Gus" is gone!—[Sobbing, he pulls out his Red Silk Handkerchief, and applies it to his eyes]

Bessie Ferguson. [With her face turned away, she sobs immoderately]

Archibald Ferguson. [Turning to his Daughter—in tremulous tone] My Child!—who will you have for "Protector"— when your Brother is gone to the "War."—

Bessie Ferguson. [Looking Heavenward—then, with tear-stained face turning to her aged Father—in tone of affected confidence] I'll have you, my dear Father!— [Sobbing violently, she buries her face on his breast]

Archibald Ferguson. [Protectingly throwing his arms over her—abstractedly—in deliberate, sorrowful tone] No— my Child—I didn't want to live to see this War!—

Bessie Ferguson. [Looking up at him—in eager tone] Will it be a long "War," Father?—

Archibald Ferguson. [In grave assuring tone] It will, my Child—be a great "War!"—and before it is ended, the Land will be filled with "Soldiers' Widows and Orphans!"—and "Soldiers' Mothers" lamenting the loss of only Sons!—and "Soldiers' Sisters" bewailing the loss of only Brothers!—

Bessie Ferguson. [Impatiently looking Rear—in poignant tone of grief] How can I part with my only Brother!—[Sobbing violently, she buries her face on her Father's breast]

Archibald Ferguson. [Protectingly throwing his arms over his distressed Child, he bows his head, contemplatively]

Captain Ferguson. [With hasty step he enters by Right Rear.—Looking across the apartment, he assumes a

gesture of surprise, and suddenly halts. Looking
Front—in a tone of satisfaction—Aside] They think I
have gone!—and what a beautiful Picture of Resignation!—[In exultant tone—Aside] I am spared the terrible ordeal of "Leave-Taking!"—[With light step hastily
going and getting his Satchel, and with it hastily starting toward Right Rear—halting and dropping his
head—in tremulous tone—Aside] But I must not leave
without my Father's Blessing!—[Turning round and
looking toward her—in confiding tone—Aside] And my
devoted Sister's Prayers may prove the Amulet that
would keep me unharmed through many a bloody
field!—[With light step he goes and sets back Satchel,
and with firm step starts toward his Father and his
Sister]

Bessie Ferguson. [Bounding toward him—in joyful tone] My
dear Brother!—[Rapturously embracing him] Why
didn't I hear you come in!—[Taking hold of his hand,
and leading him toward him] Your dear Father is long-
ing to see you—

Captain Ferguson. [Bounding into the seat beside him, and
seizing the extended hand—in tone of deep affection]
My dear Father!—

Archibald Ferguson. [Looking dotingly at him—in subdued
tone of parental authority] My "Dear Boy!" I want a
little of your company before I let you leave me.—
Indeed, I want a good deal of it.—[In grave tone] And I
have a few words of advice to give you, my Dear Boy—
for your guidance, when your old home—with its hal-
lowed influences – is far behind you!

Captain Ferguson. [Looking admiringly at him] My dear
Father! your advice has ever been—and shall ever
be—law to me!—

Archibald Ferguson. [In tremulous tone] Never has a Father
been more blessed with a dutiful son!—and I'm proud of
my "Dear Boy!"—[Bowing his head, he sobs violently]

Captain Ferguson. [In emphatic earnest tone] The principles
instilled into my mind, from my youth—by precept and

example—by you, my dear Father!—and with which I
have won the confidence and esteem of my fellow-citi-
zens of all classes—of this my native town—shall be
my principles—my only principles—in a service in
which Inhumanity, Mercilessness, Violence to the finer
feelings of the heart, and all Uncharitableness, may be
the highest recommendation to promotion!—

Archibald Ferguson. [In tone of satisfaction] Then, you will
not come home to me, my "Dear Boy," a great "General"—[Pointing illustratively to his breast—in tone of
condemnation] with your breast *without*, decorated with
dazzling "Stars"—[Darting at his breast, his forefinger--
in sarcastic tone] but *within*—to your grave—tortured
with poignant "Recollections" of the savage deeds of
warfare to which you should owe your distinction!--

Captain Ferguson. When the work shall be finished, for which
I quit, today, the more congenial pursuits of private
life—

Archibald Ferguson. [Eagerly—in assumptive tone] You will
put up your sword, my Boy, and head your Command
for home.—

Captain Ferguson. [Pointing Right Rear, and with his arm
motioning upward] When our Flag shall be reinstated
in its former high places throughout the land—

Archibald Ferguson. [In positive tone] The "War" should
then be at end, my Boy—

[From Off, Right Rear, comes the thrilling air of
"Rally Round the Flag, Boys," immediately followed
with an outburst of loud cheering]

Captain Ferguson. [Rising, and backing, a step—in tone of
patriotic determination] When the bold bad men who
sacrilegiously lay violent hands, today, [Pointing back,
Right Rear] upon the "Stars and Stripes," shall be
chastised for that high offence, until they are able to
fight no more; and sore at heart and maimed in limb,
they lay down their arms and sue for peace—

Bessie Ferguson. [Looking earnestly up at him—in commis-
erative tone] To return to ruined homes!—

Archibald Ferguson. [Earnestly looking up at him—in confident tone] You wouldn't help the rascally "Politicians" to run them down, then, in a merciless "Raid" of "Plunder"—

Captain Ferguson. [Looking down at his Father—in emphatic tone] It is cowardly--it is infamous, to persecute a conquered people!"—

Archibald Ferguson. And should one of their exacting "War Measures" make the rash utterances of Southern women, an offence punishable with incarceration—

Captain Ferguson. [Looking assuringly down at him—in earnest tone] Let her be friend, or let her be foe, I will ever be found ready to befriend a woman in distress!— I hold in too much reverence, [Reverently glancing Heavenward] my sainted Mother's Sex, to ever assist to deprive a Spirited woman of her independence!—[In sarcastic tone of condemnation] And a Ukase so barbarous!—so unworthy of our Country!—so unworthy of our Age!—should be avowedly disobeyed by at least [Deliberately pointing to himself] one "Loyal" Union Soldier!—

Archibald Ferguson. [With the aid of his staff, promptly rising, and heartily embracing him—in tremulous tone of deep affection] You shall have your Father's "Blessing," for your "Protection," my "Dear Boy!"—

Bessie Ferguson. [Going up to him, and looking admiringly up at him—in earnest tone] And your Sister's Prayers [Reverently looking Heavenward—in solemn tone] shall ascend for you, dear Brother!—Morning, Noon, and Night—until you return home to her!—[Sobbing, she throws her head upon his shoulder]

[Suddenly, from Off, Right Rear, comes a thrilling "Marching" air on a Bass Drum, approaching, immediately followed by the heavy tread of "Marching" Troops]

Archibald Ferguson. [Excitedly looking Right Rear, he looks at his Son]

Captain Ferguson. [Looking significantly at his Father, he sadly bows his head]

Archibald Ferguson. [Looking distressingly up at him—in tremulous agonizing tone] Is my "Dear Boy" leaving me—so soon!—[Sobbing violently, he throws his head upon his shoulder]

Captain Ferguson. [Looking sadly at his Sister and his Father, violently sobbing—with heads bowed upon his shoulders—looking at audience—in indignant sarcastic tone] My dear Country has been grossly insulted by her "Disloyal" Sons!—who have [Throwing up his arm and violently motioning it downward] pulled down from its high place—[Stamping the floor] and trampled upon it— [A large Starry Banner, borne aloft by a stalworth Blue Coat, shows at Middle Rear, slowly passing from Right to Left]

Captain Ferguson. [Turning round and pointing admiringly Rear] Her glorious and unsullied Flag!— [A Fife and Drum Band playing "Rally Round the Flag, Boys" is passing close behind

Archibald Ferguson. }
Bessie Ferguson. }   [Violently sobbing, they seize firm hold on him]

Captain Ferguson. [With bowed head looking at his Sister and his Father clinging to him—in deliberate sorrowful tone] It is to help to chastise the red-handed authors of that unpardonable outrage, [The "Oldham Blues" suddenly show filing past with heavy measured tread] That I must now sever the strong ties that bind me to this dear Home!

[Citizens—with noticeably grave demeanor—show passing behind the Oldham Blues]

[Tableau]

[End of Scene IV.]

[END OF ACT I.]

IN ENCORE:

Captain Ferguson. [With bowed head, and Handkerchief to his eyes, he slowly backs Rear]

Bessie Ferguson. [With her gaze fixed on her departing Brother, she leads her Father—tottering, and leaning on his staff—toward Sofa, Left]

ACT II.

SCENE I. [New Orleans. Esplanade Street. Louis Daponte's House. A large Drawing-Room. Right Rear and Left Rear, open Doors. At Middle Rear, wide open Door. Left, a little Front of Middle, an open Door. Against wall, Left, Front of open Door, a Sofa. Through Middle Rear, Steamboats show passing from Left to Right] [Off, Left Rear, a Brass Band is playing "Dixie's Land"]

Louis Daponte. [A New Orleans merchant. Of average height, and slightly corpulent. Above fifty, but of erect stature, and in a well preserved condition. In a becoming every-day suit of clothes, with hasty step entering through Middle Left, and with arm demonstratively raised, turning Front—in caustic tone of warning] Let them fire their first shot at that Sacred Banner—that received its baptism of blood, as it was triumphantly carried from Bunker Hill to Yorktown, by their patriotic ancestors—and as if by magic, enemies will rise up to them throughout the world, in the mailed friends of human freedom!—

Harry Daponte. [A little above the average height, and of lithe, but muscular and compact frame. Looking about twenty-five.—In a becoming every-day suit of clothes, he excitedly enters through Right Rear]

[A volley of joyful exclamations comes from
Off Right Rear.]

Louis Daponte. [Promptly turning round, he looks Rear]

Harry Daponte. [Going up to his Father—with a gesture of Horror—in grave tone]   South Carolina has already struck the initial Sacrilegious Blow!—[Hanging his head—in tone of regret] and her gallant Sons are the first to rise in arms against their Country!—

Louis Daponte. [In sarcastic taunting tone] That distinction can not sully the escutcheon of that Old Hotbed of "Rebellion!"   [With a gesture of horror facing Front—in soliloquy—in tone of condemnation]   Her "Flag" insulted on her own soil!—fired at!—pulled down from its high place at one of her wide Gateways—where it was a Beacon lighting the way to the "Land of Liberty!" — pulled down [Stamping the floor] and trampled upon!—[In indignant exclamatory tone]   By whom!—by her ancient foe!—[In grave tone]   Humiliating Confession—no—no—but by those who should ever be found ready to defend it!—[In tone of mortification]   by her own Sons!   [In emphatic tone of condemnation] by her own degenerate Sons!—[With head bowed, he excitedly strides Rear.]

Harry Daponte. [Approaching his Father, a step—in confident tone]   The success of the Rebels would be sad "News," Father, to the down-trodden millions of the Old World, for it would deprive them of the Asylum irrevocably offered them in the rising Free Republic of the West.—

Louis Daponte. [Advancing—in emphatic confident tone] The "Dissolution" of the "Union"—that would open to our jealous so-called "Mother Country," and to other rapacious Nations, a tempting field for the exercise of subtle measures of conquest abroad — would be promptly signalized throughout their dominions, by the despotic rulers of the Earth, with the forging of New Chains on their subjects!

[The joyful exclamations Off, Right Rear, are repeated]

Blanche Daponte. [Of lithe symmetrical figure well above the average height—with an intellectual handsome

face that is a happy compromise between that of the
Brunette and that of the Blonde, and with a wealth of
long glossy dark Hair. Just out of her "Teens." Wearing a "Janty Hat and Feather," with a blood Red Sash
thrown negligently over her left shoulder. With
bounding step entering by Left Rear, and with smiling
face approaching her Father and her Brother—in clear
musical tone] Judging by the excitement of the pop-
ulace in the streets—where the Bankettes and Crossings
are blockaded with surging masses of men of all classes
in their Shirt sleeves, and Merchants and Draymen can
be seen franticly embracing each other—the Election
of a "Radical" President has greatly "fired" the "Southern Heart"—ha! ha!—[Pointing back] And Canal street
—near Clay Statue—is the scene of a clamorous Mass
Meeting, addressed from a Stand above which I could
see waving [In sarcastic tone] every Flag—except one—
[Turning away—looking back—in emphatic tone] that
I wanted to see there! —

Louis Daponte. [In chiding tone of parental authority] Be
careful, my Child!—how you express yourself at the
present time!—

Blanche. [Promptly facing her father] I don't care who
hears me! [Approaching him, a step] I don't care who
knows it—I like that Old Flag!—I like it for its glorious history!—on Land and on Sea!—[She petulantly
turns away, and starts toward Sofa]

Louis Daponte. [Excitedly approaching her, a step—in stern
tone of Command] Blanche! [Stamping the floor] I
repeat, Blanche!—you must tone down!

Blanche. [Turning round—in tone of resentment] What
must I tone down for, Father!—[Approaching him, a
step] or is it for my outspoken devotion to one Flag!—
and that [Withdrawing from the folds of her Dress, and
deliberately unfurling it—a silken Striped Banner stud-
ded with glittering Stars—and facing the audience,
and patriotically waving it aloft before her—in tone of
admiration] the dear "Flag" of my Country!—

[The Band promptly plays the "Star Spangled Banner"]

Blanche. [Turning round, with independent bearing she strides Rear]

Louis Daponte. [Following her—in serious soothing tone] When passion is reason, my Child!—and the will of the "Mob" is the Rule of the hour—

Blanche. [Folding her Banner, and setting it down against the wall, Right, near Rear, she poutingly approaches her Father]

Louis Daponte. [Significantly nodding at her] And it may become your duty, my Child, as well as your Father's—

Blanche. [Looking submissively at him—in petulant remonstrating tone] Should we have "War," I, too, may be a Red-Hot Rebel.—But until the Secessionists commit some overt act of Treason—that would rouse the North—

Louis Daponte. [Looking gravely at her] The "Rubicon" has already been crossed, my Child!—and we must now prepare for "War!"—for "War" in its worst form!—

Harry Daponte. [In assuring tone] And the insolent Gage thrown down by the South Carolina "Nullifiers," will not remain long unanswered by the brave Men of the North!—

Cadwallader Jacobs. [A blustering City "Swell"—wearing a high Hat and Kid gloves. Tall and lubberly, and about Thirty.—Bounding in, Right Rear—in tone of contempt] "The brave Men of the North!"--[With swaggering gait advancing—in arrogant tone] I can "Whip" a "Half Dozen" of the "Mudsills"—myself!—[Halting, and looking from one to the other of the gentlemen— in earnest, chiding tone] Our *best* people are at this moment holding enthusiastic "War Meetings" throughout the City. And I hope that you, gentlemen, are not defending the cowardly "Abolitionists," [Assuming a soldierly bearing] when *we* are getting ready to give them a good trounsing.

Blanche. [Scornfully turning away, she seats herself on Sofa]

Louis Daponte. [Looking rebukingly at him] Young man!—
when Louisiana determines to draw her sword, it
will be time enough for her Loyal sons to offer her
their services. [He scornfully walks away]

Harry Daponte. [Approaching him, a step—in rebuking tone]
Granting that our State will draw her sword in the
Cause of Southern Independence, where—tell me—
might you be seen helping to whip the Yankee "Boys
in Blue," when we should be seen fighting them at the
"Front"—[In taunting tone] or is it in the ranks of a
skulking "Home Guard!"—

Louis Daponte. [Promptly turning round—in serious tone]
When their natural "Protectors" would be away in the
Tented Field, my Son—vindicating the honor of the
Pelican State—[Significantly looking at his Daughter]
our young women may, on some occasions, be in need
of "Protection."—

Cad Jacobs. [Bowing his thanks—in arrogant tone] And
they should have it, in "Guards" officered by Gentlemen—[Assuming an aristocratic bearing] by young
Gentlemen of high social standing—native and to the
manor born [Throwing out his aristocratic foot] to
boot—[With smiling face looking across at her—in
confident tone] Don't you think so, Miss Daponte—

Blanche. [Bounding to her feet, and scornfully looking across
at him] Sir! we "Creole" Girls are no cowards! And
should our gallant Fathers and Brothers leave for dis-
tant fields—to fight for us—we should commit ourselves
to a "Protection" more acceptable to us, than that of
"Home Guards"—[In taunting tone] "Officered by Gentlemen:" [Vehemently stamping the floor] we should
be our own "Protectors!"—[With heroic bearing she
turns round, and resumes her seat]

Louis Daponte. [Looking contemptuously at him] My
Daughter has not yet caught your "War" spirit—and
she believes with me, that our State is not yet ready to
commit herself to the fatal heresy of "Secession."—

Cad Jacobs. [Approaching him, a step—in assuring tone]

The "People's Convention" meets within an hour, and yours is the only important House on Carondelet Street that will not be represented there.—I am a Delegate. [Striking a warlike attitude] And all of us true "Southern Boys" want to "fight"—want a chance to "pepper" the "Yanks"—ha! ha!

Blanche. [Promptly rising, and bowing to her Father and her Brother, with erect bearing and deliberate step, she departs by Middle Rear]

Louis Daponte. [In sarcastic tone] In a time of peril, it is in her Fields and in her Workshops that the pulse of a gallant Nation can be felt!—[Turning away—looking back—in sarcastic tone] not in her Broker Shops— where it never beats!—

Harry Daponte. [Approaching him, a step—in sarcastic tone] Cad Jacobs! how many, think you, of those doughty "Cotton Kings" who will be rampant "War Men" at your Meeting today, would shoulder their Muskets to participate in the bloody conflict to which they would commit their State!—

Cad Jacobs. [In emphatic assuring tone] All of them.—

[The joyful exclamations Off, Right Rear, are repeated]

Cad Jacobs All of them, most certainly—[Suddenly turning away, he departs hastily, by Right Rear]

Louis Daponte. [Looking at his son—in serious tone] The unprincipled demagogues who are engaged in the outrageous work of throttling this State, will not hesitate to employ any means within their reach, for the achievement of that undertaking!—And to save us from a "War" in which we should have so much at stake, let us do what we can—[Hastily going through open Door, Middle Left, and immediately returning with his Hat and Cane—in tone of determination] let us raise our Voice against it!

[The joyful exclamations Off, Right Rear, are repeated in increased volume]

Harry Daponte. [Looking Right Rear—looking seriously at his Father—in confident tone] It wouldn't surprise

me if we should find "Rotunda Hall" the scene of a
turbulent assemblage—with its deliberations dictated
with their bludgeons, by a despicable minority!—

Louis Daponte. [Testing his Sword Cane, and feeling his
Pistol Pockets—in serious tone] We have a high duty
to discharge at that Convention, my son!—[With hasty
step, he starts toward Right Rear]

Harry Daponte. [Feeling his Pistol Pockets, and with hasty
step starting after Father—suddenly halting and look·
ing Front—in thrilling tone of determination] And
if in its discharge we fall, we shall not fall alone!—

[End of Scene I.]

Scene II. [New Orleans. A Street along a dilapidated Old
Red Brick Wall]

[Enter, Right and Left, and running past, men of all
classes—in thrilling tone shouting] "War!"—"War!"—

Dennis O'Flynn. [A broad-shouldered, well sunburnt Irish
Levee Laborer, of average height, and about 35—in
Blue Overalls and Red Flannel Shirt, and gaily wearing an Old Panama Hat—smoking a short Clay Pipe—
with deliberate step entering Right—soliloquizing—
in serious tone] They're goin to "War" agin the
North—and there'll be no "Levee" wurk this year.—
[In confident tone] And they'll want me to "fight"
with them.—[Halting, and assuming an attitude of
meditation—and scratching his head—in serious tone]
I don't want to be fighting agin me Brother Barney—
who settled down among the Yankees, the day he
landed at Castle Garden—twenty years ago.—[Assum-
ing a pugilistic attitude] But I was agin the "Union"
in Ireland—bad luck to it!—I mane the "Union."—
[In emphatic tone] And I'm agin it still!—and "fight·
ing" agin it is the only wurk in sight now for me.—
[Adjusting his Hat, and assuming a soldierly bearing
—in exultant tone] And maybe I'll come back from
the "War," a "Kurnel"—[Thrusting his hands into his
Overalls Pockets, and assuming an arrogant bearing] to

live loike a Gintleman the rest of me days - and whin
I'm dead, to be "waked" in good style by the "Boys,"
and be honored with a foine monument, by the warm-
hearted South.—[With soldierly bearing, and bounding
step, he proceeds on his way, through Left Entrance]

[End of Scene II.]

SCENE III. [Scene I, repeated]

Blanche. [Excitedly bounding in by Left Rear—in tone of
disappointment] Where are they all!—[Going Front—
in tone of astonishment] Grave Business Men can be
seen running along crowded streets, shouting aloud,
and franticly gesticulating, as if they had lost their
reason!—[Pointing Left Rear] And from the Gallery, I
could hear a great clamor [Pointing Right Rear] in the
direction of Rotunda Hall—

[The merry Ringing of a Church Bell comes from
Off, Right Rear]

Blanche. [With a gesture of surprise—in confident tone]
Saint Peters' Bell!—

[The merry Ringing of a Church Bell comes from
Off, Middle Rear]

Blanche. [Looking that way] That's Saint Johns!—

[The merry Ringing of a Church Bell comes from
Off, Left Rear]

Blanche. [Excitedly looking that way] The Synagogue's
Bell!—[Assuming a gesture of astonishment] What
does it all mean!

[The merry Ringing of Church Bells comes now from
all directions]

Blanche. [In soliloquy—in confident serious tone] They must
have heard some joyful "News"—

Caesar. [A Coal Black Colored Waiter, out of breath, bounding in, Left Rear—in tremulous tone] Dere is a great
Fire, Miss Blanche!—somewhere.—[Running toward
her] But dere is no "Smoke," Miss Blanche!—

Blanche. [Pleasantly looking at him] They are "Firing" the
"Southern Heart," Caesar—ha! ha!

[The startling report of a discharged Cannon comes from Off, Right Rear]

Caesar. [Thrown off his feet by the shock] Dat's a 'Splosion, for sure!—

Blanche. [In soliloquy—in confident tone] "F ring" Cannon over their "News"—

Caesar. [Hastily starting toward Left Rear, looking toward Right Rear] I is afeard of dem 'Splosions—

[The startling report of another discharged Cannon comes from Off, Left Rear]

Caesar. [With a gesture of terror turning round] De good Lord have Mercy on dis Colored sinner!—[He excitedly bounds through open Door, Left]

Louis Daponte. [He shows entering by Right Rear]

Blanche. [Looking around Front—in tone of satisfaction] Now, I'll know what these great rejoicings are all about.—[Bounding toward her Father—suddenly halting—and with a gesture of alarm looking at him—in tone of anxiety] My dear Father! what means that haggard altered look!—what has gone wrong!--[Anxiously looking Rear—in impatient tone] Where is my brother!—

Louis Daponte. [In halting serious tone] The "War Meeting" broke up in a Row—

Blanche. [Triumphantly—in sarcastic tone] Then, the "Secession" Conspirators were foiled!—

Louis Daponte. [In grave tone] But the false report got through thé City, that the State had abjured her allegiance to the "Union!"—It had instantaneous effect, and the mischief done by it was irreparable--for the Men whom it influenced to bound from their places of business, and from their homes—and who could be seen running blindly past—were not in a reasoning mood.

Blanche. [With a gesture of Horror—in sarcastic tone] That wicked report was the work of the Conspirators, in their desperation!

[The firing of a Minute-Gun comes from Off, Middle Rear]

Louis Daponte. [Excitedly pointing Rear—in grave assuring tone] And the "News" is now flashing through the land!—

Blanche. [With a gesture of Horror backing, a step—in startling rebuking tone] That Love of Country has ceased to "fire" the hearts of "Louisianans!"—[Laying her hand over her heart—in emphatic tone] which I proclaim to the world, an unmitigated falsehood!

Louis Daponte. [In serious assuring tone] 'Tis astonishing, my Daughter, what "Preparations" they had been making—[In confidential tone] making in secret!. -

Blanche. [In tone of astonishment] "Preparations" to "fight!"—

Louis Daponte [Approaching her, a step—in enthusiastic tone] And so well equipped are our brave "Creole Boys," to strike a Blow for "Southern Independence," that our First Regiment—the "Grays"—

Blanche. [With a gesture of surprise—in tone of satisfaction] The "Grays"—

Louis Daponte. [In emphatic enthusiastic tone] The "Crescent City Grays"—needs but a few hours preparation to take the field—

[An "Assembly" call comes from Off, Right Rear]

Louis Daponte. [He looks intently, that way]

Blanche. [With a smiling face, promptly looking at the audience—in enthusiastic tone] I like the "Gray!"—I like the *Color*—

Caesar. [Bounding in through Left Rear—in tremulous tone of alarm] Robber in de House, Miss Blanche!

Blanche. [With a gesture of Horror—in tone of alarm] A "Robber!"—

Caesar. [Running Front past his Master—turning round] Robber in de House, Master!—

Louis Daponte. [Looking back at him] Where is he!--where is he!—

Caesar. [Pointing Left Rear] He's in young Master's Room! —

Blanche. [With a gesture of Horror, she looks Left Rear]

Caesar. [Pointing to his shoulder] And he has "fixins" up here on his Coat. —[In tremulous confident tone] He's a Robber, sure, Master!—

Louis Daponte. [In tone of raillery] Ha! ha!—you'd make a poor Soldier, Caesar—

Louis Daponte. [Looking round at her] I'm not afraid of that Robber—[In determined tone] and I'll go and capture him!—[He starts toward Left Rear]

Caesar. [Calling to him] Don't let him shoot you, Master!—

Blanche. [Bounding after him] Before he can shoot my Father, he'll have to shoot me down!—

Louis Daponte. [Turning round and motioning her back] That "Robber" is your Brother—in his "Gray" Uniform—gone to his Room to pack his Trunk—and I'll bring him in here to you.

Caesar. [With a gesture of Surprise—in soliloquy—in serious tone [Young Master goin to de "War!"—[Bounding Left Rear—looking back] Now, I isn't afeerd of dat "Robber"—ha! ha!—

Blanche. [With a gesture of astonishment, looking Front—in soliloquy—in serious tone] My patriotic Brother in a "Rebel" garb!—What has so suddenly turned his head— and induced him to take side against his Country!—[In sarcastic tone] What if his native State has arrayed herself against the "Union"—[With emphatic reverent tone] the "Union" that he loves!—[Assuming an attitude of contemplation] And what occasion did he have for putting on the "Gray," with such undue haste—[In confident tone] or did he fear that [Pointing to herself] his patriotic Sister would oppose his espousal of a Cau·e which she knew that he at heart condemned!— [Assuming a listening attitude, and looking eagerly Rear--looking around Front--in confident tone] And perhaps he doesnt want me to meet him in his "Rebel" Uniform!--[With determined bearing, and hasty step, she starts toward Left Rear]

[End of Scene III.]

Scene IV. [New Orleans. Esplanade Street. Louis Daponte's House. A wide Hall, formed by a Partition across the Stage, in Front of Sofa. Right and Left, closed Doors show in Partition. Open Doors at Right and Left.]

Captain Daponte. }
Louis Daponte. } [Conversing seriously, with deliberate step they enter together, by Right Entrance]

Captain Daponte. [Harry Daponte, in the "Gray" Uniform of a Confederate Captain – with head bowed, entering in the lead—in soliloquy—in apologetic serious tone] I had to choose between my State and my Country—

Louis Daponte. [With head erect, addressing him—in tone of satisfaction] With a home to defend, and a hearth to guard, it would be cowardly for us, my Son, to look with folded arms, on all that was dear to us exposed to imminent danger!—And when our State joined hands with her elder Sisters—in a common Cause—it would make us unworthy descendants of illustrious sires—would cast upon our proud name, an indelible stigma—to enlist under the Banner of the "Invader!"—

Captain Daponte. [Languidly pointing back—in captious tone] If those people at Montgomery know their business, an advance movement in force, without delay—to put the enemy on the defensive—is among their military projects.

Louis Daponte. [In ostentatious tone] To judge them by the completeness of their "Preparations" for the "Conflict, my Son—

Captain Daponte. [Facing Front—looking right back at his Father—in sarcastic tone of rebuke] Those "Preparations" are the dark Work of Years!—the Work of cowardly Conspirators!—[In sarcastic tone] the kind of men to whom many a Nation owes its downfall!—to whom not one owes its uprise!—[Turning away, he deliberately walks, Left]

Louis Daponte. [In sarcastic retorting tone] But they are not older than the Provocations that justified them!—

[Following him, a step] And the Collision was but the work of time—the inevitable result of the enemy's assaults upon our "Institutions!"—

Captain Daponte. [He assentingly drops his head]

Louis Daponte. [In emphatic assertive tone] And the boldness—the impunity with which her "Abolition" Societies have been robbing us of our property, makes the North, the "Aggressor!"—

[An "Assembly" call comes from Off, Right Rear]

Captain Daponte. [Promptly starting Right—suddenly Halting, and looking at his Father—in tone of uneasiness] But I should take leave of Blanche!—

Louis Daponte. [In tone of warning] If you don't want her to follow you—

Captain Daponte. [With a gesture of Horror—in earnest tone] No!—No!—I don't want my innocent Sister to come in contact with the Associations of my Camp— and be compelled to listen to the ribald jests of Citizen Soldiers!—[Looking significantly at his Father—in grave tone] And it is not without solicitude for her safety, that I turn my back upon Blanche in this City, to-day!

Louis Daponte. [Looking pettishly at him] But think, my Son—think if you can—of the greater indignities to which your Sister would be exposed—of the greater dangers that would threaten her safety in this City— on account of its military occupation—should it be triumphantly entered by the enemy, and its homes be subjected to the surveillance of the insolent subalterns of a Licentious Army!—

Captain Daponte. [Dissentingly turning away—turning back in sarcastic tone] I have never subscribed the estimate of Northern Valor generally received at our side of the "Line."—And show me a brave people, and I will show you a gallant people.—With these convictions, I can not—[With startling emphasis] and I will not— subscribe any estimate that impugns "Northern Gallantry!"—[Petulantly turning away, with independent bearing he walks off, Left]

Louis Daponte. [In sarcastic tone] "Money Making" is not a brave people's principal Occupation!—[In malicious tone] And you don't know the "Psalm Singing" Cutthroats of whom you speak!—

Captain Daponte. [Turning round, and looking composedly across at him—in serious warning tone] But it will take more than bluster to resist the march of a Patriot Army!—

[A "General" Call comes from Off, Right Rear]

Captain Daponte. [In tone of mortification] The "Grays" are moving!—[With hasty step, he departs, Right]

Louis Daponte. [With a gesture of Horror looking around at audience—in sympathetic tone] And he will not be able to meet a Sister that he idolizes!—[With hasty step, he follows him through Right Rear]

[End of Scene IV.]

Scene V. [Same as Scenes I and III]

[Off, Right Rear, a Fife and Drum Band is playing "Dixie's Land"]

Blanche. [Her "Janty Hat" falling back on her head, and her beautiful long Hair disheveled, bounding in through Middle Rear—eagerly looking around—in tone of distress]—Where have they gone!—[Bounding up to Centre Table, and eagerly picking up a Photograph Case, and looking critically at the Picture—in tone of satisfaction] His Likeness—in an Officer's Uniform. [In pouting tone] But he must not leave me, in that shabby way—[Petulantly throwing it down, she bounds out in direction of Music]

Captain Daponte. [Off, Middle Rear, approaching] I must meet her!—[Hastily entering—suddenly halting—in tone of mortification] She's not in the House!—

Blanche. [Off, between Right Rear and Middle Rear—in loud tone of displeasure] Wait till I catch the runaway!—

Captain Daponte. [Rapturously looking Rear] She's coming!—[Looking right back at audience—in exultant tone] And once more I can look upon my dear Sister's beautiful face! [Through Middle Rear, he impatiently bounds out of sight]

Blanche. [Off, Middle Rear—in loud upraiding tone] You naughty Brother!—[Bounding in—by the hand pulling him after her—in triumphant tone] You were again trying to steal away from me!—[Advancing with him] But you are now my Prisoner—[In jeering tone] ha! ha! [Halting him, and from head to foot surveying him—in tone of satisfaction] My brave "Soldier Boy!"—

Captain Daponte. [Tenderly taking her by the hand and drawing her up to him—in tremulous grave tone] I wanted to look upon my dear Sister—once more!—

Blanche. [Looking devotedly up at him—in tremulous tone] I believe I know what my dear Brother wants to say to me!—[Weeping, she buries her face on his breast]

Captain Daponte. [In hoarse tone] Blanche! you were the last of whom I wanted to take "Leave!"—

Blanche. [Earnestly looking up at him] I hope, dear Brother, that you have given due attention to your "Leave-Taking."—

Captain Daponte. [In assuring tone] I have "called" upon a number of dear "friends"—Young and Old.—[Looking significantly at her—in earnest tone] My Sister! I will never exchange the trusty Old friends I know, for the New ones I have not tried.

Blanche. [In tone of exultation—Aside] I will put to a severe test, his Secession Zeal.—[Looking seriously up at him—in confident tone] There is one very dear Old Friend of whom you have not yet taken "Leave"—

Captain Daponte. [Unpleasantly looking down at her—in petulant tone] I havent the time to do it, now, my Sister—but who is he?—who is he?—

Blanche. [She bounds toward Right Rear]

Captain Daponte. [He looks intently after her]

Blanche. [Picking up the Starry Banner that she had put away there, and quickly unfurling it, and holding it aloft, and with a smiling face looking across at him—in reverent tone] And this is that dear old "Friend!"—

Captain Daponte. [He guiltily hangs down his head] [Promptly, a Fife and Drum Band playing a "Rebel" air, and Troops "marching" with firm tread, are heard approaching, Off, Right Rear]

Captain Daponte. [Over his left shoulder—in urgent supplicatory tone] Blanche! please, put that down!—[With head bowed, and slow step, he starts toward Left Rear.— Suddenly turning round, he looks intently across, and reverently bows to the Old Flag] [The Band of the "Grays," playing their "Rebel" air shows slowly at Middle Rear]

Blanche. [Vigorously waving aloft her Starry Banner, she bounds before Middle Rear] [The patriotic "Band Boys" promptly halt, and bowing to the Old Flag, play the "Star Spangled Banner."—Turning away, they proceed Left, marching to the tap of the Drum] [The Color-bearer of the "Grays," with head erect showing passing, he promptly turns round, and "dips" his Standard] [As with bounding step the "Grays" show passing, each of them turns round, and bows reverently to the Old Flag]

Captain Daponte. [Sadly turning round right, and facing Front—in soliloquy—in desponding confident tone— Aside] What a serious blunder—that they didn't adopt the "Old Flag!"—[With head bowed, and slow step, he departs through Left Rear]

Blanche. [With slow step going Front, with her Flag held aloft, and looking at audience—in grave confident tone] The sight of the "Old Flag" across their path, will unnerve—[In emphatic tone] will paralyze the upraised arm of many a one of our brave "Boys!"—

[Citizens following behind, show joyfully passing]

Blanche. [Glancing Rear—furling her Banner, looking pleasantly at audience—in tranquil tone] I, too, will go and bid a merry "God Speed" to the brave fellows, as they leave—[Pulling out her White Pocket Handkerchief, and putting it to her eyes—in tremulous predictive tone] many of them never—never to return Home!

[End of Scene V.]

[END OF ACT II.]

ACT III.

SCENE I. [New Orleans. Esplanade Street. Louis Daponte's House. Part Front of the House—shown on Left of Stage. Part of House out of sight, Left. The Second Story Windows show Shutters closed.—Time—just before the Occupation of New Orleans, by the Federal Army.]

Caesar. [With high Hat, Kid Gloves, and Cane—with bounding step entering, Right—facing Front, and assuming a pugnacious attitude] When Old Master was goin to de "War," he left a "Pertector" to Young Mistress, when he left dis "Nigger" to "tend to de Door"—and "do de Errands."- And if any of dose "Home Guard" fellows —who are goin about insulting ladies—gets into dis House—[Drawing out a long White-handled Razor] it will be over de dead body of [Pointing to himself] Mister Julius Caesar Jackson![—Putting back his Razor] I don't want Young Mistress to know dat I carries a Razor—what every "fighting" Coon carries— yah! yah!—[In confident tone] 'Tis too early for Young Mistress to be down stairs.—[Looking Front—in spiteful tone] And I'll go and give a good "cussing" to some of dose Virginny "Niggers" down in Shanty Street,

who are praying for de Yankees to land. [With bounding step, departing by Right Entrance, he pulls out his
Razor, and brandishes it, aloft.]

[End of Scene I.]

SCENE II. [New Orleans. Esplanade Street. Louis Daponte's
House. A large Parlor. The Walls are hung with
"War" Maps. A Confederate Flag Stands out from
Wall, Right, near Rear. Open Doors at Middle Right
and Middle Left. Wide Open Door at Middle Rear. A
Centre Table, a little Left. A large Open Window,
Left, Front of Middle. A Sofa, Left, Front of Middle.
Chairs at Front, Left of Centre, and nearly in line with
open Window]

[A mournful military air comes from
Off, Right Rear]

Blanche. [In dark morning Robe—a Pink Sash thrown loosely
over her left shoulder—her beautiful long Hair falling
disheveled down over her back—her beautiful face very
pale, and wearing an expression of weariness—entering
through Middle Rear, and with slow step advancing
Front—in soliloquy—in grave positive tone] It is
known that a number of decisive Battles have been
fought!—[Turning to Centre Table, and languidly ex-
amining its contents—in tremulous tone] And had we
the News of our losses, many a happy home to-day in
this City, would be a scene of disconsolate mourning!—
[Weeping, she puts her Handkerchief to her eyes]

[The measured heavy tread of Troops "Marching,"
comes from Off, Left Front]

Blanche. [With hasty step going up to Window, and looking
intently out—in tone of satisfaction] I can see from my
Window, the bronzed faces of gallant fellows in "Gray"
marching past—

[A Troop of "Boys in Gray" are seen passing outside,
at a quick pace]

Blanche. [Looking after them—in languid confident tone] I
live in a Confederate Stronghold, and am within hailing

distance of friends.—[Suddenly, with head bowed turning right, and listlessly gazing around the apartment—
in piercing tone of loneliness] But the solitude of my
home is never broken by the presence of a dear face!—
by the thrilling tone of a dear voice!—[Looking around
Right Rear—in despairing tone] by a familiar footstep
in the Hall!—[Looking around Left Rear] or by the
violent knocking at the Door, [In emphatic eager tone]
of the bearer of hasty "News" from the dear ones!—
    [Off, Left Rear, the Door Bell rings]

Caesar. [Without Gloves and Cane—his high Hat crushed,
and his Black Coat all torn—bounding in, Right Rear—
in hilarious tone] Ha! ha!! ha!!!—[Suddenly halting, he.
hangs down his head]

Blanche. [Calling to him—in petulant tone] Caesar!—

Caesar. [Pulling off his Hat, and bounding toward her] Here
I is, Miss Blanche—

Blanche. [Looking critically at him] You've been fighting —
[Pointing Left Rear] But go—answer the Door Bell—

Caesar. [He bounds away Left Rear]

Blanche. [Anxiously looking Left Rear—in grave confident
tone] No—no—my present lonely situation—with its
anxieties—its burning longings—its apprehensions—its
dangers—didn't fully occur to my dear Father, as he
was leaving me behind him, in this City!

Caesar. [He returns, without delay, and promptly proceeds
toward his Young Mistress]

Soldier. [In the guise of a Confederate Private Soldier, a tall
and muscular gentleman, with a well-bronzed intellectual face—looking about 30—with military tread and
bearing, enters, Left Rear. Suddenly halting, and looking Front, he pulls off his Cap, and deferentially bows
to the lady]

Blanche. [In petulant tone] Who is this fellow you have ad-
mitted—and what's his business here—[Motioning him
Rear] But go—lead him this way—

Soldier. [Under lead of Caesar, he unobtrusively advances.
Front]

Blanche. [In tone of satisfaction – Aside] He has the bearing
of a gentleman, if he is a "Private" Soldier.—And he
has a prepossessing look.—[Motioning him to retire] If
I need you, Waiter, I will call for you.—

Caesar. [By way of Right Rear, he promptly retires]

Blanche. [Setting a Chair, and affably motioning him to the
seat] Please be seated.—

Blanche. [Drawing to her a Chair, and seating herself—facing
him—at a proper distance—pleasantly looking at him—
in eager firm tone] Soldier, what is your business in this
House?—I hope you are the bearer of good "News!"—

Soldier. [Excitedly looking around—confidentially bending
toward her—in subdued earnest tone] If you have any
VALUABLES in this House—any JEWELRY—GOLD COIN—
and SILVER WARE—[He looks excitedly around]

Blanche. [Recoiling from him—Aside] The fellow's a Robber!—and to get possession of my Jewelry, he would
take my life!—[Excitedly looking Right Rear—in
lusty loud tone] WAITER!—WAITER!—

Soldier. [Looking intently at her—in subdued earnest tone]
GET IT ALL TOGETHER!—to the meanest Silver Spoon!—
[Confidentially bending toward her—in tone of mysti-
fication] for he would take that too from you!—
[He looks uneasily around]

Blanche. [With a gesture of alarm, looking Right Rear, with
straining eyes—in stentorian tone of distress] WAITER!—
WAITER!—WAITER!—[In great agitation—Aside] Am I
shut up in the House all alone with him!—

Soldier. [Intently looking at her—in subdued earnest tone]
AND HAVE IT CONVEYED WITHOUT DELAY—[Critically looking around at the open Doors] TO A MORE SECURE PLACE
FOR IT!—[Looking admiringly at her—in serious assuring tone] And this House will not be a SECURE QUARTER
for yourself!—[He looks uneasily around]

Blanche. [With a gesture of surprise—in tone of satisfaction—
Aside] I begin to think that he meditates no harm to
me.—[Confidently looking at him—in eager tone]

Soldier! what is this imminent danger of which you kindly warn me!—

Soldier. [Anxiously looking around—in subdued grave tone] The disclosure may cost me my life!—

Blanche. [In earnest tone of alarm] Then, you know of some terrible Ordeal to which my present situation exposes me!—

Soldier. [Uneasily looking around—confidentially inclining his head toward her—in subdued serious tone] Your City is the destination of a formidable military Expedition—that may at this moment be advancing upon it!—under a mercenary and merciless Commander!— And today, it has no Andrew Jackson, to go out and beat back the Invader!—and once more save it from the "Sack" of an imbruted Soldiery intoxicated with a dearly bought victory, let loose upon it!

Blanche. [In a tone of alarm] Mercy!—

Soldier. [Bounding to his feet, he looks uneasily around at the open Doors]

Blanche. [Excitedly rising, and with a gesture of Horror looking at him—in tone of distress] What will become of us defenceless "Creole Girls!"—

Soldier. [Looking back—in subdued assuring tone] "Forewarned" is "Forearmed"—[With hasty step departing, Left Rear—looking back at her—in tone of alarm] I am lost if I loiter here!—

Blanche. [Looking admiringly after him—in emphatic serious tone] A splendid fellow!—whoever he is.—[Turning left, and assuming a gesture of meditation—in serious tone] What notice should I take of his warning—that this House is not a safe place for my "Valuables!"—nor for Myself!—[In confident tone] He's a "Friend"—[In serious tone] and I should improve my opportunity—before that terrible "Spoon Thief" and his myrmidons are ransacking the City!—[She bounds through open Door, Middle Left]

[End of Scene II.]

SCENE III. [New Orleans. A Dark Street, dimly lighted with
Gas, from Lamps out of sight, Right and Left]

[Blue Coat Private Soldiers, triumphantly shouting in
maudlin tone, enter Left, and with unsteady step cross
the Stage, and disappear, Right]

["Reveille" comes from Off, Right]

[From Off, Left, in a Voice of terror, comes the startling Cry] P-O-L-I-C-E!—P-O-L-I-C-E!—

A Citizen. [Bareheaded, with Coat all torn, and face chalky
white—a corpulent little gentleman bounds in through
Left Entrance, out of breath, and suddenly turning
round, with a gesture of Horror looks back]

[A thrilling avenging Shout comes through Left
Entrance]

A Citizen. [Promptly turning round, he departs, Right, as
fast as trembling legs can carry him]

Captain Ned O'Harra. [A burly broad-shouldered Irish Federal Officer—a little above the average height—with a
broad well-colored face, and Grayish dark Hair]

Captain Clem Fury. [A Federal Officer—looking about 40—
of athletic, symmetrical frame—well above the average
height, and with prepossessing look]

Private Mickey McCarthy. [A broad-shouldered, shock-
headed Irish Blue Coat Private—of average height, and
about 40]

[Promptly, the three Blue Coat Soldiers show at Left
Entrance—Captain O'Harra, between Captain Fury and
Private McCarthy—who are holding him back]

Captain Fury. [In tone of reproof] The gentleman was peace-
ably passing when you assaulted him!—

Private McCarthy. [In a mild scolding tone] He didn't spake
a word to you, Captain—

Captain O'Harra. [His high black Hat thrown well back on
his head, and noticeably well dented. His Hair disheveled over his forehead. His Nose noticeably large, and
of a flaming Red. In maudlin petulant tone] Didn't
he insult me, Mickey—

Captain Fury. No—he didn't Captain.—He only pointed to your Nose—

Captain Fury.
Private McCarthy. } [In hearty gleeful tone] Ha! ha!! ha!!!

Captain O'Harra. [In penitential tone] And you say I knocked him down for it—

Capta:n Fury. [In grave assuring tone] After you began to "load up," Captain, you seemed to have lost respect for all persons!—

Captain O'Harra. [With a gesture of Horror, looking at them —in tone of uneasiness] Have I insulted a woman!—

Captain Fury.
Private McCarthy. } [In emphatic exculpating tone] No!—No!—

Captain O'Harra. [In exultant tone] Now, I'm not ashamed of anything I have done!—

Captain Fury. [In confident tone] Then, you don't remember that you were at the "Theatre Burgundy"—

Captain O'Harra. [Looking brazenly at him] But I behaved myself properly there—[In confident tone] didn't I—

Captain Fury.
Private McCarthy. } [In hearty gleeful tone] Ha! ha!! ha!!!

Captain O'Harra. [He looks aghast at them]

Captain Fury. [In serious tone] You appeared to know all the pretty Women in the Auditorium—and to be on intimate terms with all the pretty Actresses—judging by your rapturous notices of them as they came on the Stage—when you could be heard from Pit to Gallery, endearingly calling them by "Pet" Names—

Captain Fury.
Private McCarthy. } [In hearty jeering tone] Ha! ha!! ha!!!—

Captain O'Harra. [Hanging his head, he turns away, and confidently facing the audience—in sonorous exculpatory tone]

What wonder if blunders one makes,
When Whiskey has turned his poor head:

More wonder how few his mistakes,
When he is out [Pointing to his Nose] "Painting
   it Red."

When to the Theatre one goes,
He must come home with [Pointing to it] a
   swelled head:
And he must expect [Pointing to it] a Red Nose,
When he stays out "Painting it Red."

If I was in Camp, you could see
Me *saintlike* now [Snoring aloud] snoring in bed:
But how a full Saint could one be
When he is out "Painting it Red."

When I was in Ireland at School,
I would be [Trying to look learned] a "Statesman,"
   they said:
A Statesman looks like an Old Fool,
When he is out "Painting it Red."

[Turning right, and pointing joyfully toward Right
   Entrance—in tone of satisfaction]

There's a place by yon Light I think,
Where "Wretches" are "liquored" and fed;
And where a chap can get a "Drink,"
Who has been out "Painting it Red."

   [Starting—looking back Front]

Then, why should a fellow be glum,
When he could be merry instead.—

   [Proceeding with unsteady step]

And sober home how could one come,
When out all Night "Painting it Red."

Captain Fury, }
Private McCarthy. } [Departing close behind—in hearty
   tone] Ha! ha!! ha!!!

         [End of Scene III.]

Scene IV. [Scene II, repeated]

> [A Brass Band is heard playing a thrilling National
> air, Off, Left Rear]
>
> [The Door is heard savagely kicked, Off, Left Rear.—
> Immediately, it is heard falling in]

Ben Adamson. }
Blake Stansbury. } [In "Provost Guard" Uniforms—with
Swords drawn—they bound in through Left Rear]

Private O'Murfie. [An athletic Irish Blue Coat Soldier—of
average height—and about 40—armed with a Musket,
he bounds in at the heels of the Officers]

Ben Adamson. [Looking back—in commanding tone] Guard!—
[Pointing to Doors at Rear] you will let no one pass
out—[Pointing to Middle Left] while we go through
the House.—[He daringly leads the way]

Blake Stansbury. [Promptly bounding after him—in exultant tone] "Beauty and Booty"—ha! ha!

> [The startling Reports—in close succession—of two
> Pistol Shots, immediately come from Off, Middle Left]

Ben Adamson. }
Blake Stansbury. } [Off, Middle Left, lustily shouting together—in tone of distress] Murder!—Murder!—

> [Through Middle Left—in a ringing feminine voice—
> comes the startling Command] Go back!—Go back!—

Private O'Murfie. [Looking toward Middle Left—in tone of
satisfaction] Them "Daisy" Officers have caught a
"Tartar"—ha! ha!—

> [Off, Middle Left—from a nearer point—in blood-
> thirsty tone] Go back!—Go back!—

Ben Adamson. }
Blake Stansbury. } [Hurriedly backing together, into the
apartment—hands raised in abject supplication—both
together—in tone of entreaty] Dont shoot, again!—
Dont shoot, again!—

Private O'Murfie. [Looking contemptuously across at them—
in gleeful tone—Aside] They cant stand the smell of
"Powder"—ha! ha!

Blanche. [Following in, in close pursuit—in a dazzling Red
Silk short-sleeved loose Sack—with a Silk tricolored
little Cap firmly set on her well-poised small head, and
holding in place her beautiful Hair falling straight
down her back—her white arms bare to the elbows—
and firmly holding in her small white hands, a brace of
ferocious White-handled Revolvers, at full cock, determinedly pointed at the heads of the scampering
"Provost" Officers—in tone of rebuke] Go back!—
[Backing them across the Room—in tone of indigna-
tion] How dare you follow a lady—[In exultant tone] a
Southern lady—to her private apartments in her own
House!—

Ben Adamson. }
Blake Stansbury. } [Quaking with terror—both, together—
in piteous tone of supplication] Lay down those ugly
things!—do, please!—

Blanche. [Resolutely holding them at Bay—in taunting tone]
Who are you?—and what's your business here?—Speak!—
I'll let you speak for yourselves, if you are my "Pris-
oners"—ha! ha!

[Immediately, "Troops" are heard approaching by
way of Middle Rear]

Ben Adamson. [Looking bravely at her—in authoritative
tone] Our Orders are to seize your "*valuables*," and take
them to "Head-Quarters"—

Blake Stansbury. [Looking seriously at her—in assuring
tone] For "*Safe Keeping*"—

Ben Adamson. And should we find you refractory—to take
Yourself there!—

Blanche. [Looking scornfully at them—in triumphant tone],
My "*valuables*" are now well beyond your reach!—[In
earnest tone of gratitude—Aside] Thanks to my
"Strange Soldier Friend!"—[Brandishing at them, her
formidable weapons—and with her little foot vigorously stamping the floor in tone of defiance] *And you*
can't take myself!—

Lieut. Phineas Prig. [A young Blue Coat Officer, with a blooming cheek—he bounds in through Middle Rear]

Sergeant Morris. [A Stalworth Blue Coat Orderly—he enters immediately behind, with a Squad of Blue Coats]

Ben Adamson. [In sarcastic tone] We'll soon have enough help to take you along!—

Blanche. [Looking Rear—in earnest tone] Those brave men are "Soldiers"—who would not insult a woman!— [Charging upon them] But you are no "Soldiers!"— You are no "Gentlemen!"—

Sergeant Morris. [He tears down the Confederate Flag and replaces it with the "Stars and Stripes."]

Ben Adamson. }
Blake Stansbury. } [They precipitantly retreat to the Protection of the line of "Blue Coats]

[The Band promptly plays the "Star Spangled Banner"]

Blanche. [Dropping her arms to her sides, she looks triumphantly after the "Scampering" Provost Officers.]

Lieutenant Prig. [Superciliously stepping forward] So this is the little "Tigress" that the General wants to see.-- [Conceitedly advancing toward her—in pleasant confident tone] I guess I can take this [Smiling familiarly at her] pretty Prisoner along –[Deliberately raising his arm, as he approaches her] *all by myself—*

Blanche. [Backing, a step –in sarcastic tone of rebuke] Lay not your foul hand on me!–[Backing, a futher step, and raising a Cocked Revolver, and with a steady arm taking deliberate aim at his head—in startling tone of defiance] Sir!—at your peril!—

Lieut. Prig. [Suddenly backing away—in tone of supplication] Don't, please!—Dont—[He hurriedly backs Rear]

Sergeant Morris. [With modest bearing, he starts toward the fair Prisoner]

Lieut. Prig. [In confident tone—Aside] Those beautiful "Creole Girls" will shoot!—I didnt believe it before.—

Blanche. [Going toward him, a step—in firm respectful tone] Soldier!—

Sergeant Morris. [He promptly halts]

Blanche. I will facilitate, as much as possible, your discharge of your unpleasant duty. [Dropping her arms to her sides, with rapid firm step she goes up to Orderly, and submissively hands to him, her weapons.—Backing, a step, and looking contemptuously at her Captors—turning left and looking back Front at audience—in incisive ironical tone] It should receive high complimentary mention, in the bright Record of the great Yankee Army of "Occupation"—an Exploit in which it took [Turning back and pointing at them] but a Squad of "Picked Men," [Pointing at them—in jeering tone] and their *brave* "Officers," [Turning left, and again looking at audience] to take to Prison [Pointing to herself—in triumphant tone] *one* spirited Southern Girl!

Sergeant Morris. [With his Men, he promptly advances upon her]

Blanche. [With a gesture of astonishment, backing—looking rebukingly at Orderly—in tone of indignation] What's the need for this demonstration of brute force!— [Quickly turning right round, and bounding Front—in soliloquy—in tone of condemnation] Has it come to this, to save the "Union!"—

Sergeant Morris. [With his Men, he promptly follows her—halting at a respectful distance]

Blanche. [Turning half round, right, and deliberately pointing to Banner at Rear—in earnest tone] I have ever been an admirer of the Old "Flag!"—[Pointing vaguely, Off, Right, and with a gesture of Horror backing, a step—in sarcastic rebuking tone] and its desecration over there, [Violently stamping the Floor] I have never ceased to condemn!—[Looking impressively at her Guards and their Officers—in emphatic declaratory tone] "Secession"—whose Standard has been followed from an early day, by all who are dear to me, on Earth— has never had in me, a hearty Supporter!—[Petulantly turning left away, and assuming a bearing of independence, and looking right back—in tone of indignation] But when the privacy of Southern Homes must be outrageously violated—and spirited Southern Women must be persecuted and degraded—*as means for preserving it*—the "UNION" instituted for a *Blessing*, proves to our beloved Southland, *an Odious Association!*—

Sergeant Morris. [With his Men, he proceeds to surround her]

Blanche. [Violently stamping the Floor—in startling sarcastic tone] And it can not be "Dissolved" too soon—for me!

[Tableau.]

[End of Scene IV.]

[END OF ACT III.]

IN ENCORE:

Blanche. [Surrounded by her Guards, she quickly faces Front, and withdrawing from her bosom, a Miniature Confederate Flag, spitefully waves it aloft]

ACT IV.

SCENE I. [Belair Plantation. Madame Robart's House. A well furnished Parlor. A Shady Lawn shows through two wide open Doors at Rear. At Middle Right and Middle Left, open Doors. A Centre Table. A Sofa, at Centre— well to Front of Middle. A Confederate Flag runs out from Wall, Left, immediately Rear of Middle.]

Madame Robart. [A matronly looking lady of symmetrical, well developed figure—above the average height. Of typical 'Creole" complexion. Wearing the conventional "Widow's Cap." With a profusion of dark shining Hair falling in rolls down over a pair of round shoulders. With leisure step entering through Middle Right—in soliloquy—in serious tone] My greatest anxiety now is about Brother Louis's Daughter—left all alone in a Bar-

rack of a House!—[In chiding tone] It was a great
mistake of her Father—when he was going to the
"War"—that he didn't send her here to me.—Blanche is
Nineteen, now—and she must be a fine Girl. [In tone of
solicitude] And many eyes· are set upon her, in the
City.—[Looking Left Rear—in petulant tone] It is high
time for those Girls to be back.—[In cynical tone] It
will not be a minute—after they get their eyes on those
young Camp Officers—before they carry them off with
them—out of my sight!

Blanche. [Through Right Rear, she shows slowly approaching through the Lawn]

Amy. [A pleasant-faced young lady of lithe figure--a little
above the average height—in gay outdoor Dress—with
long dark Hair falling loose down over her back]

Josephine. [A pleasant-faced young lady of symmetrical
figure—well above the average height—in gay outdoor
Dress—with long dark Hair falling loose down over
her back]

Amy. }
Josephine. } [With smiling faces, they leisurely enter together, through Left Rear, and advance Right Front—
toward Madame Robart]

Madame Robart. [Hanging down her head, and turning right
round Front—in soliloquy—in tone of self-reproach]
They were sent here to me—to take care of them!

Blanche. [In a well-faded Traveling Dress, her beautiful long
Hair falling disheveled down over her back, and wearing a plain Janty Hat—with slow step she enters from
the Lawn, and advances]

Amy. }
Josephine. } [Looking Right Rear, they suddenly halt—in
ecstatic tone] 'Tis Cousin Blanche!—[They eagerly
bound toward her]

Madame Robart. [With a gesture of surprise, she turns round]

Amy. }
Josephine. } [Rapturously kissing her] We thought—long
ago—that you were dead—that some dreadful fate had
befallen you!—

Madame Robart. [Eagerly going up to her and embracing her—looking kindly at her—in sympathetic tone] You look fatigued, my Child—

Amy. [Looking up at her] And hungry, Aunt Louise!—

Blanche. [Looking at them—in startling tone of earnestness] I am *Starving!*—

Madame Robart. [With a gesture of Horror] Go, Josephine! and bring her some refreshment!—until Dinner is ready—

Josephine. [She bounds through Door, Middle Left]

Amy. [She bounds for a Chair, and sets it for her]

Josephine. [She immediately returns with a huge Tray loaded with dainty refreshments]

Amy. [Bounding up to Centre Table, and carrying it toward Blanche] You need a Table for your Tray, Josephine—

Josephine. [Setting Tray before her] I hurried back to you, Cousin Blanche—with a Luncheon—

Blanche. [With gloating eyes surveying the repast] You live well here—

Amy. But you were not without luxuries down in the City, Cousin Blanche—

Blanche. [Not raising her eyes off the tempting viands before her] They robbed us of everything they could get their hands on!—[With both hands she seizes a bone of Cold Turkey, and ravenously raises it to her Mouth]

Madame Robart. [With a gesture of Horror turning away—in grating tone of rebuke] The Robbers had her nearly starved to death!—[In tone of gratification] And she hasn't come to me a minute too soon!—

Amy. [From a Bottle, drawing the stopper, and pouring out a Glass of Wine] All "Creole" ladies drink Wine—

Blanche. [Eagerly seizing the Glass, and taking a couple of generous sips] How I did miss my Claret!—

Amy. We are dying to hear your account of your long incarceration by the "Blue Coats," Cousin Blanche—

Madame Robart. [In sarcastic tone] And of her narrow escape from the Robbers—with her life!—

Josephine. [Bounding to back of her Chair, and holding up her beautiful long Hair] And with all of her beautiful Hair, Aunt Louise!

Blanche. [In ridiculing tone] Of what use could my Hair be to them!

Amy. }
Josephine. } [In positive tone] To send it home—with your Jewelry—to their Sweethearts and their Sisters—

Madame Robart. [Looking assentingly at Amy and Josephine— in serious tone] I heard it, myself—that the Yankee Robbers were doing some dirty work of that kind, down in the City—

Amy. [Looking assuringly at her] The "News" was, Aunt Louise, that when the "New Commander"—"General Beast"—Something—

[Immediately, a huge Cock·Eye Likeness shows for a moment, at Rear]

had seized all the Coin and Silver Ware—to the last "Silver Spoon" on which he could get his hand—and shipped it home North, he commenced a shocking per.secution of his helpless victims!--

Blanche. [Dropping the bone she was picking, and assuming a gesture of Horror—Aside] The half of it can never be told!

Madame Robart. [In sarcastic tone] What more could the Monster take from them!—except their lives!—

Amy. [In grave assuring tone] Their "Hair," Aunt Louise!—[Pointing to that of Blanche] their beautiful Hair!—And the "News" was, that of that sacred personal orna-ment, "General Beast"—Something—

[Immediately, the Cock-Eye Likeness shows again, for a moment]

was stripping all the beautiful "Creole" Girls he could find within his lines, and shipping it North, by the Cargo!

Josephine. [In confident tone] To be worn by his Northern School-Madams—

Madame Robart. [In cynical tone] No—no—for their Horse-Hair "Switches" are good enough for them!—

Blanche. [Rising, and pointing to herself] I can point to one "Creole Girl" who would resist unto death, so outrageous a liberty with her person!—
[She resumes her seat]

Amy. But it is true Cousin Blanche, that they took from you, your "Jewelry" and "Silver Ware"—

Blanche. [Looking exultingly up at her] I had timely warning of the danger that threatened my "Valuables"in my own possession—

Amy. [In congratulatory tone] Then, you had a "Friend" within the enemy's lines!—[In confident tone] in a "Confederate Spy"—

Blanche. [Looking pleasantly at her—in assuring tone] I had a "Friend" in a mysterious Visitor, who, I fully believe, was a "Federal Spy"—

Amy.
Josephine. } [With gestures of surprise turning round—in tone of satisfaction] A "Blue Coat" "Spy" befriended her, Aunt Louise!—

Madame Robart. [With a gesture of Horror looking at her.] What did you say, my Child!—that you met a "Friend" in a "Yankee Cutthroat!"—[Turning away—in tone of alarm—Aside] I believe in my soul, that the Robbers frightened the poor Child out of her reason!—and sent her to me, a complete wreck!—

Amy. [Looking pleasantly down at her—in confident tone] Your escape through the Yankee lines must be a thrilling adventure, Cousin Blanche!

Madame Robart. [Looking kindly down at her—in sympathetic tone] Surely, the Robbers didnt keep my poor Child all the time locked up in their Jails—

Blanche. [Looking languidly up at her] I was kept a close Prisoner in my own House, Aunt Louise—[Suddenly rising—in indignant tone] and I could bear no longer, the insulting surveillance to which, by order of the brutal New Commander,

[The Cock-Eye Likeness shows for a moment, at Rear]

all spirited "Creole Girls" were subject!

Amy. [Looking admiringly at her] And in your desperation, you made a bold break for Belair—and Liberty—

Josephine. [In tone of banter] With the connivance of a friendly "Blue Coat" Guard—ha! ha!—

Madame Robart. [Pointing to Confederate Flag] We are now within the Confederate Lines.—[Pointing Right Rear] But we have for a near neighbor, a "Blue Coat" Bull-Dog—with a large force at his command—who wants to frighten us to death, with his savage visits—
                    [Musketry Firing, Off, Right Rear]
Amy. }
Josephine. } [With gestures of alarm looking Right Rear] Mercy!—there's a fight at the Picket Line!
        [The fighting is heard fast coming nearer]

Major Perkins. [In hoarse bloodthirsty tone] Shoot them down!—Shoot them down!—

Madame Robart. [With a little Shriek, fainting, she drops on the Sofa]

Amy. }
Josephine. } [They run Left Front, where, cowering with fear, they turn round]

Blanche. [Turning round, and looking rebukingly after them] Stand your ground!—and by your womanly courage, cheer your brave Defenders!—

The "Grays" [Enter, Right Rear, on the "Double Quick," Confederate Soldiers, who suddenly stand and turn round, and "Club" their Muskets]

The "Blues." [Enter, Right Rear—in close pursuit—on the "Double Quick—shouting triumphantly—Blue Coat Soldiers with "Clubbed" Muskets]

[The "Blues" and the "Grays" fight desperately, to and fro, across the Stage, and out Left Rear]

Confederate Orderly. [Sword in hand, and with blood-stained face, he bounds in Right Rear—on the run—and out, Left Rear]

Major Perkins. [Approaching—in bloodthirsty tone] Dont let
one of the Traitors escape!—[A robust muscular Blue
Coat Officer—well above the average height—Gray-
haired—with ruddy face, and savage look – in disarranged Uniform, with sword drawn, he bounds in,
Right Rear—and looking savagely Front, he suddenly
halts.—His eye falling on the Confederate Flag, he
eagerly bounds up to it, and savagely tearing it down—
in vindictive tone] We'll take along this vile sectional
Standard!—this "Flaunting Lie!"—for a small Trophy—
[Unfurling the Starry Banner that he carries] and re-
place it with the glorious Standard of an Invincible
Nation!—[Erecting it, and looking admiringly up at
it—in emphatic confident tone] The great Flag of the
Future!—the Flag of an Emancipated World!—

> [The Band promptly plays the "Star Spangled
> Banner"]

[Savagely looking at the ladies, he quickly turns away,
and retreats by Right Rear]

Blanche. [Looking up at the "Stars and Stripes," and with a
gesture of Horror backing, a step—turning right—in indignant tone] Am I again under the odious "Yankee
Flag!"—[Backing, step further] And did I escape from
one Federal Prison, to flee to Another one—for
Refuge!—

Amy. ⎫
Josephine. ⎬ [Bounding up to her, and looking inspiringly
at her—in rallying tone] We promise you lots of fun at
Belair, Cousin Blanche—if you go with us—[Seizing
her by both arms, and bounding Rear with her—in tone
of excessive jolliness] ha! ha!—[Suddenly halting, they
talk confidentially to her, in undertone]

Madame Robart. [In tone of dissatisfaction—Aside] The im-
pudent little Simpletons have already taken full charge
of her!

Amy. ⎫
Josephine. ⎬
Blanche. ⎭ [Intently engaged in merry conversation in
undertone—in loud hearty tone] Ha! ha!! ha!!!

Madame Robart. [In curt commanding tone] Blanche!—

Amy.
Josephine. } [Seizing hold of Blanche, and bounding out of sight with her—in loud hearty tone] Ha! ha!! ha!!!—

Madame Robart. [Looking Front—in tone of mortification] They are trying to turn that innocent girl against me!—[In sarcastic tone] to infect her mind with their romantic notions—with the delights of "Fishing Parties"—which catch no "Fish!"—and "Moonlight Excursions"—when there's no "Moon!"—and I can't take her from them, too soon!—[With hasty step following them—her eye falling on the "Stars and Stripes"] This is my House—[Pulling down the hated Flag, and replacing it with a Confederate Flag] and this is my "Color!"—[With proud bearing, she proceeds on her way, departing]

[End of Scene I.]

Scene II. [Fort Union.—Entry way to the Fort, Left.]

[A Squad of "Blue Coats" carrying Muskets, headed by an Orderly Sergeant, enter by Left Entrance, in single file, and with measured step crossing the Stage, depart through Right Entrance]

Captain Ned O'Harra. [With bounding step entering by Left Entrance—looking left back] Sorry to lose your companionship, Captain Fury—

Captain Clement Fury. [He deliberately enters close behind]

Captain O'Harra. [Halting and turning round—in tone of satisfaction] But the "War" will soon be over, Captain Fury—when all of us "Regulars" will be messing together again, at our old Posts on the Frontier.—

Captain Fury. You are not near enough to the source of patronage, in the present War, Captain O'Harra—to be favorably noticed for your gallant services.—

Captain O'Harra. [In emphatic confident tone] It was unfortunate for "Little Mack," that he was too near to Washington City, to escape the interference of a meddling War Department. The same may be said of that

distinguished soldier of two Wars—General Shields.
And it was most fortunate for Grant, that when his Star
was ascending, he was too far away for officious interference with his movements.—If Great Soldiers are
made at Washington, Captain Fury, Great Soldiers are
also *slaughtered* there!--[In exultant tone] And I am
glad that I am stationed more than a thousand miles
away—where, for "getting Drunk," or for "winking" at
a pretty woman, and such like indiscretions—"ungen-
tlemanly conduct"—ha! ha!--I should be in no danger
of being "court-martialed," and of having my long term
of unrewarded service brought to a close—by a dis-
graceful cashiering. [Confidentially approaching him, a
step] Have I ever told you, Captain Fury, that I had a
Lady-Love living not many miles from here—

Captain Fury. This is the first I have heard of it, Captain—

Captain O'Harra. [In exultant tone] A Charming Widow—
childless—and "well fixed."—No, I haven't told you—
[Taking him by the arm, and with leisure step leading
him toward Right Front—in jovial tone] and I wouldn't
tell you, now, if you were not going away—ha! ha!—I
had a clear field, and I didn't want to give away a good
thing. And if my suit materializes, my old Brothers-
in-Arms will have a pleasant place at which to stop
over, on their Furloughs.

[Through Right Entrance, a number of "Blue Coats,"
armed with Muskets, bound in, helter-skelter, hurrah-
ing, and bounding across the Stage, disappear through
Left Entrance]

[End of Scene II.]

Scene III. [Belair Plantation. Madame Robart's House.
Scene I, at its close]

Madame Robart. [In a well-fitting Black Dress—showing a
well-compressed waist and symmetrical figure—with
elastic step entering through Middle Right, and
promptly looking to Right Rear.—Sadly turning away,
and looking toward Left Rear—in tone of dissatis-
faction] 'Tis now two whole weeks since that Girl came

to me—and I have not yet had a minute of her company.—[Turning Front—in soliloquy—in desponding tone] And one of these days—when the "War" is over, and "Refugees" are returning to their Homes—they will all be leaving me!—[In tone of anguish] It is terrible to be living all alone!—[In self-accusing tone] And 'tis all my own fault!—in my "Weeds" buried away in this House—instead of "fixing up" and going abroad, and passing for what their cosmetics pass, now-a-days—at the "Springs"—[With smiling face looking over the audience] and at the Theatres—ladies many years my elders—a "Charming Young Widow!"—

[An explosion of hearty laughter, in loud sonorous tone, comes from the Lawn, Off, Right Rear]

Madame Robart. [She looks gladly that way]

Captain O'Harra. [From a nearer point—in thrilling Irish Brogue]

> In War or Love we can't be beat,
> For an Irishman the world all over,
> Is the bravest Soldier you can meet—

[Bounding in from the Lawn, an Armless Sleeve dangling at his right side—with a Nose noticeably large, and of a flaming Red, and gaily wearing his Cap on one side]

> And an Irishman is the boldest Lover.—

Ha! ha!! ha!!!—

[He suddenly halts and makes a ludicrous Salam]

Madame Robart. [Promptly advancing to receive her visitor — in cordial tone] Always welcome to Belair, Captain O'Harra—ha! ha!—

Captain O'Harra. [Seizing the extended White hand, and cordially shaking it] I was thinking of you, Madame—and couldn't pass your House without Calling—

Madame Robart. [Setting a Chair for him—in tone of gratification] You were thinking of poor me, Captain O'Harra—

Captain O'Harra. [Throwing himself into the soft seat, and looking back at her] An open confession is good for the Soul, Madame—ha! ha!—

Bud Talbot. [Through Left Door Rear, a Confederate Scout is noticed emerging into view, and with stealthy step crossing the Lawn—in a Left Rear direction]

Madame Robart. [In pleasant bantering tone] Then, you Soldiers will sometimes go out of your way, to call upon "Pretty Women"—tehee—[She bashfully hangs her head]

Captain O'Harra. [Promptly looking up at her] *I* will always do it, Madame.—[Bounding to his feet, and looking seriously at her] It is when he is thinking of his Sweetheart, that the Irish Soldier always has his best inspiration to fight.—And that's why his charge is always so irresistible, Madame, when he goes into Battle to the always dear music of "The Girl I left behind me."—

Madame Robart. [She is giving him marked attention]

Captain O'Harra. [Bending confidentially toward her] I've composed some Poetry about You, Madame.—It was my first effort in that line.—[Facing Front, and throwing forward his chest, and clearing his throat—looking seriously around at her] The Poets first composed, when they were "head and heels" *in love.* [Throwing forward his Chest, and again clearing his throat—in rich barytone]

> Had I again my bachelor life,
> Before me all to go over,
>> [Glancing around at her]
> The world should to-day have one more Wife—
>> [Pointing to himself]
> And it should have one less Rover.

Madame Robart. [Looking significantly at the insignia of his rank—in facetious tone] According to my thinking, Captain O'Harra, there should be one less "Captain," and one more "General," to-day, in the Yankee Army.—

Captain O'Harra. [Looking seriously at her—in emphatic tone] The "Volunteer" Officers—with their political influence—stand in the way of us "Regulars," in this "War."—And all of them want to be "Generals" or high up "Colonels." — [Abruptly turning away—looking pleasantly back] You flatter me, Madame.—

Madame Robart. [Looking admiringly at him] Why is it, Captain O'Harra, that in all the great Battles of the world, the Irish Soldier fought, generally, on the stronger side?—

Captain O'Harra. [In tone of satisfaction] Ha! ha!—[Pointing to himself] The Irish Soldier, Madame, generally makes the stronger side.—

Madame Robart. [In serious, confident tone] Then, it is because they have brave Irishmen to do their hard "fighting," that the Yankees have not been "whipped"—long ago—by our brave "Boys."—

Captain O'Harra. [In blunt tone—Aside] There may be a few grains of truth in that view of it.—[Looking pleasantly at her] The Yankees have never been "Whipped," Madame!—And if they have England and his Satanic Majesty against them, they have with them, gallant Old Ireland and great Jehovah!—And they can't be whipped in their present fight, Madame—[In bantering tone] ha! ha!—

Madame Robart. [Shrugging her shoulders] That's only *Your* Opinion, Captain O'Harra!—

Captain O'Harra. But that's my firm conviction, Madame—for with the propagation of an odious type of human bondage, for the Corner-Stone of your "Cause," Madame, [Pointing reverently upward] they are solid against you, up there!—[In emphatic tone] And there is not enough Power *down here* to make yours the stronger side!—

Madame Robart. [She dissentingly turns away.]

Captain O'Harra. [Looking pleasantly across at her] You don't agree with me, Madame—ha! ha!—[Backing away, obsequiously bowing to her] And I don't want to have my first quarrel with you—ha! ha!—

Madame Robart. [Looking around—in conciliatory tone] But I am not yet tired of your *company* Captain O'Harra.

Captain O'Harra. [Pointing back] The "Fort" is my Post of duty at the present moment, Madame—[Formally bowing to her, he turns quickly away, and with hasty step departs through Right Door into the Lawn]

Madame Robart. [Looking after him—in pettish tone] He went away displeased with me!—And I had no business to talk "Politics" to him—what a Soldier never wants to hear—and what we Women know nothing about.—[Assuming an attitude of meditation] He's not young—and he's not handsome.—But he is brave!—and he has young ways—[Bashfully hanging her head] like myself—tehee.—[In a tone of mortification] I didnt go to the Door with him—and I didnt tell him Come again!—[With hasty step starting Right Rear—suddenly looking back—in exultant tone] He'll be looking back—[Merrily waving her White Pocket Handkerchief] and I'll be merrily waving to him.

[End of Scene III.]

SCENE IV. [Belair.—A shady Glade leading immediately into an impenetrably dark Thicket, Left]

[From immediately Off, Right Entrance, comes in chorus, in a feminine animated strain]

"Uncle O'Harra"—"Uncle O'Harra"—

Amy. [In a Gay Dress with a fantastic Hat]

Josephine. [In a Gay Dress with a fantastic Hat, which she wears gaily]

Blanche. [In a rich Gay Dress with a black fantastic Cap ornamented with a blood Red Tassel]

Amy.
Josephine.
Blanche. } [Hands joined, with leisure step they enter, and gaily facing Front—in hilarious tone]

And he has the "Cut" of a Born Rogue—
Uncle O'Harra—Uncle O'Harra.
And he is Irish—and has the Brogue—
Uncle O'Harra—Uncle O'Harra.
And he has a "fighting" rakish way,
And he has Hair that is Silver Gray—
He is Four Score, if he is a day—
Uncle O'Harra—Uncle O'Harra.

The clumsiest Bridegroom he would make—
Uncle O'Harra—Uncle O'Harra.
His Bride to his *arms* he could not take—
Uncle O'Harra—Uncle O'Harra.
He went into Battle at Bull Run—
Which was, you know, by our brave Boys won—
With two strong arms, but there he lost *one*—
Uncle O'Harra—Uncle O'Harra.

And he could not *kiss* his charming Bride—
Uncle O'Harra—Uncle O'Harra—
Without her help—and hard work beside—
Uncle O'Harra—Uncle O'Harra.
That's what he would want to do straightway,
To his fair Bride on his Wedding-Day—
His Big *Red Nose* would be in his way—
Uncle O'Harra—Uncle O'Harra.

[In loud hearty tone] Ha! ha!! ha!!!—

[From the Thicket promptly comes, in broad Irish accent] In the Name of the United Shtates, who comes there—

Amy. [Excitedly looking at her companions—in subdued tone] We're at the Picket Line!—[Starting] Come away!—

Josephine. [She bounds after her]

Blanche. [Looking composedly after them] He's an Irish-man—and we needn't be afraid of him, if he does wear a "Blue Coat"—

[From the Thicket comes, in Commanding tone] Advance and give the Counthersign!—

Amy.
Josephine. } [Seizing Blanche, and bounding Right with her—in joyful tittering tone] Ha! ha'—

[From the Thicket comes, in determined tone] I'll make yees laugh another way—

Private McCarthy. [With Musket raised, he bounds in—looking across, he suddenly halts, and dropping his Gun, backs a step—and crossing himself—in tremulous tone] Holy Mother!—'Twas the "Good People!"—and they were laughing at me!—[Despairingly hanging his head] And maybe I'm to be kilt in the next Battle!—[Pulling out his Scapular, and reverently looking at it] It has saved me in many a "Foight!"—[Reverently pressing it to his lips, and putting it back into his bosom, and picking up his Musket, and with bowed head starting toward his post—turning round and looking Front—in tone of resignation] If I am kilt, shure I will only be following a good many of my brave Counthrymen—in a good Cause.

[End of Scene IV.

Scene V. [Belair Plantation. Madame Robart's House. Scene III, repeated]

Madame Robart. [At Middle Right, with a gesture of alarm looking Off, Right—in tone of trepidation] He's making straight for this House!—

[The Cantering of a Horse comes from Off, Right]

Madame Robart. [Suddenly pointing Rear, and sweeping her arm from Right to Left—in tone of exultation] He's taking another direction!—

[The Cantering stops, suddenly]

Madame Robart. [Looking Left Rear—in tone of anxiety] Those wild Girls are running great risks, in their rambles—with the Cutthroats prowling about!--

Amy. [She bounds in from the Lawn, Left]

Josephine.
Blanche. } [With leisure step, they enter together, close behind]

Amy. [With hasty step going up to her, and out of breath looking up at her] Aunt Louise!—we nearly got arrested by the "Blue Coats!"—[Looking chidingly back at them—in petulant tone] They wouldn't stop until we got to the Yankee "Picket Line!"—

[The Cantering of a Horse passing from Right to Left, suddenly comes from Right Rear, Off the Lawn]

Josephine. [Excitedly looking Right Rear, she nervously starts toward her Aunt and Amy]

Blanche. [Undisturbedly, she looks curiously in the direction of the Cantering]

Madame Robart. [Looking sternly at her—in chiding tone] Blanche!—are you not afraid of those Cutthroats!—

[The Cantering stops suddenly]

Amy. [In serious assuring tone] She's not a bit afraid of them, Aunt Louise!—for it was as much as Cousin Josephine and myself could do, [Glancing at her] to keep her from running into the arms of the "Blue Coat Picket!"—

Blanche. [Looking merrily across at them—in hearty tone] Ha! ha!! ha!!!—

[Suddenly— and without notice—the Head and arched Neck with flowing Mane, of a Coal Black Steed, shows through Left Door into Lawn]

Amy.
Josephine.
Madame Robart. } [With gestures of Horror, they scream]

Blanche. [Quickly turning right and looking at audience—in ecstatic tone] What a beautiful Horse!—

[The Rider—who shows only to Blanche—with his Horse, immediately backs out of sight]

Madame Robart. [With a gesture of Horror looking across at her] Blanche!—

Blanche. [With straining eyes she is looking through the Door]

Colonel Ferguson. [Captain Gus Ferguson, in a Federal Colonel's Uniform—with modest bearing he enters, and suddenly halting, looks intently at Blanche]

Blanche. [She joyfully advances, a step, and extends her
hand]

Colonel Ferguson. [Bounding up to her, he joyfully seizes the
white little hand]

Amy.
Josephine.
Madame Robart. ⎬ [With gestures of astonishment, they
look Left Rear]

Blanche. [Promptly leading him toward her company—pointing to him—in jocose assuring tone] This is that "Federal Spy"—ha! ha!—who befriended me down in the
City.—[Looking from him to her—in courteous tone]
My worthy Aunt—[Turning to them—in bantering
tone] My noble Cousins—ha! ha!—

Amy.
Josephine. ⎬ [They bow graciously to him]

Colonel Ferguson. [Looking pleasantly at her—in serious
tone] I am again at your command, Miss Daponte, to
befriend you at Belair.—

Blanche. [With a gesture of surprise looking up at him—in a
tone of astonishment] At Belair!—

Madame Robart. [In snappish tone—Aside] I'd like to know
what service the Cutthroat could render here to her.—

Josephine. [Approaching her, a step—in sympathetic tone]
Wouldn't it be nice, Cousin Blanche, if your "Blue
Coat" Soldier "Friend" was stationed at the "Yankee
Fort"—instead of Major Perkins—

Madame Robart. [Looking morosely across—in sarcastic
tone] We couldn't have that much good luck—if he
isn't Satan himself—

Colonel Ferguson. [Looking pleasantly across at her—in
hearty tone] Ha! ha!—[In sympathetic assuring tone]
You will receive no more "Visits" from Major Perkins,
Madame Robart.—He has been "Relieved" by me.—

Blanche. [Laying her hand over her heart—in ecstatic tone—
Aside] There are joys for which there are no words!—

Madame Robart. [Eagerly approaching him—in tone of solicitude] I hope you have not "relieved" our good friend, Captain O'Harra—

Colonel Ferguson. [Looking pleasantly at her—in earnest tone] A braver Soldier than Captain O'Harra, doesn't live!—He is my esteemed Chief of Staff, Madame.—

Madame Robart. [Promptly going up to him, and heartily shaking hands with him—in cordial tone] You are heartily welcome to Belair, Sir.—[Pointing to them] These Girls are my Nieces—"Refugees" in my charge. And their fancy for their "company" seems to run to "Soldiers"—ha! ha!—[Bashfully hanging her head— Aside] And mine, too—tehee.—

Amy. [Gladly looking from her Aunt to Blanche—and back— in congratulating tone] We'll have *two* welcome "Visitors" from the Yankee Fort, now—

Blanche. [Looking joyfully at them—in startling emphatic tone] We'll have *THREE!*—[Bounding Rear, and disappearing through Left Door into the Lawn, she immediately returns, leading in a caparisoned Coal Black Steed]

Colonel Ferguson. [Looking Rear, he laughs heartily]

Madame Robart. [With a gesture of Horror, looking Rear— in tone of alarm] Don't bring the *brute* in here!—

Blanche. [Advancing with him—in exultant tone] *And here is ONE of them!*—[Halting with him and patting him tenderly—in ardent tone] *I do love a fine horse!*—[Looking eagerly across at the Colonel—in inquiring tone] I hope he has a pretty Name—

Colonel Ferguson. [Looking pleasantly at her—in bland tone] APPOMATTOX—

Blanche. [Patting him caressingly—looking pleasantly up at the Colonel—in rapturous tone] Then, he's a Southern Horse!—and I like him the better for it—

Colonel Ferguson. [Looking jestingly at her—in bland assuring tone] Not since we brought him to our Side— where he gets all the OATS that he wants—ha! ha!

Madame Robart. [Looking rebukingly at Appomattox—in sarcastic tone] I don't like man or Horse—that changes his *Politics*—

Colonel Ferguson. [In hearty ludicrous tone] Ha! ha!! ha!!!—

Blanche. [Kindly patting the noble animal—in jocular tone] Ha! ha!—

[The loud ringing of a Dining-Room Bell comes from Off, Door, Middle Left]

Madame Robart. ⎫
Amy. ⎬
Josephine. ⎭ [Looking graciously at the Colonel, they step into line with him—on his right]

Blanche. [Looking pleasantly at her Horse—in companionable tone] That's our Dinner Bell, Appomattox—and you, too, must have Dinner— [Leading him to the head of the line, looking kindly at him—in pleasant assuring tone] must have what made you change your "Politics"—and what may make you change back—[Putting her mouth close to his ear—in loud tone] OATS.

[Tableau.]

[Madame Robart, Amy, Josephine, Colonel Ferguson, Appomattox, and Blanche—in the order mentioned, from Right to Left, across the Stage]

End of Scene V.]

[END OF ACT IV.]

FOR ENCORE :

Blanche. [Kindly patting Appomattox, looking at the audience—in tone of commendation] He will change back, and be a good Southern Horse again, if they dont keep giving him plenty "OATS."

ACT V.

Scene I. [CAMP CONFEDERACY. "Officers Quarters." A wide Open Door, at Middle Rear. A Field Tent—showing a Hammock—well back, Left. A Flagstaff, with the Confederate Flag flying at the top, at Rear, to Right of Middle. Through Middle Rear, a Pole with a Confederate Flag waving at top, shows at a short distance, Rear.]

Private O'Flynn. [A broad-shouldered Irish Confederate Soldier. Of average height, and about 40. Armed with a Musket, and with leisurely pace treading the Stage, at Rear, to and fro, from Right to Left—suddenly halting and hanging down his head—in soliloquy—in serious tone] The "Boys" are talking a good deal about "Home," of late.—And they are not "spilin" for a "fight" with the Yankees, anymore—those of them who are left.—And as sure as me name is Dennis—Dennis O'Flynn—the "Confedheracy" is on its last legs!—And from the President himself, down to me—who wouldn't turn "Informer," for all the Gould in England—they'll be for hanging every one of us—for "Thrayturs!" [Putting his hand to his throat, and feeling it tenderly—in serious tone] I'm awful ticklish, hereabouts—[Suddenly looking Right—immediately looking Front, and pointing Right—in tone of solicitude] A Horse coming back from the "Fight," without his Rider!—[Looking Right—with a gesture of Horror looking Front] 'Tis "Andrew Jackson!"—the Colonel's Horse!—

[A Horse is heard approaching, Off, Right Rear, at a rapid pace]

Private O'Flynn. [Dropping his Musket, and throwing up his arms] Ho!—Ho!—[Advancing—in kindly tone] Ho!—"Andy!"—[Disappearing through the Opening—immediately coming back, by the Bridle holding in check, with great effort, a raw-boned spirited Horse bedaubed with Mud—in soothing gentle tone] Ho—Ho—Andy—Ho—[Turning him round, and leading him back out—throwing the Bridle over his head, and vigorously slapping him on the back—in commanding tone]Go, now—and scramble for your Dinner—

     ["Andy" is heard bounding away, Right]

Private O'Flynn. [Picking up his Musket, and proceeding with his Guard duty—in soliloquy—in confident tone] His hollow Flanks—and bare Ribs show that "Andy" is a "True Blue" "Rebel" Horse.

Lieut. Ponsonby Blossom. [A blustering Confederate Officer—well above the average height—slightly corpulent, and with a round smooth face—about 35—with bounding step entering through Right Front, and with deliberate step, pompously going Rear—in ostentatious tone] Guard! there's not an enemy in sight.—[Noticing the Hammock, and starting toward it, and looking around at Guard, with finger pointed at Tent—in arrogant tone] And I will station myself here.—[He is noticed promptly clambering into the Hammock]

  · [A burst of startling inharmonious noise that resounds through the Quarters, immediately comes from the Tent]

⌣**Private O'Flynn.** [Looking across at Tent—a comical Grin on his face—in gleeful tone] Sleeping on Post—ha! ha!—He's a Daisy Officer—[Suddenly turning round and bounding up to Door, Right Rear, and through it aiming his Musket—in commanding tone] Halt! [Looking back] Officer of the Guard!—

Lieut. Blossom. [In petulant tone] That'll do, Guard!—[Turning away, he immediately resumes his Snoring]

Private O'Flynn. [Looking back—in impatient tone] Officer of the Guard!—Officer of the Guard!—

Lieut. Blossom. [Turning round—in peremptory petulant tone] That's enough, Guard!—Enough, I say!—[Turning away, he immediately vigorously resumes Snoring]

Private O'Flynn. [Aiming high, his Musket—in confident tone] This should bring the lubber—

[The startling report of a discharged Musket is heard through the Camp]

[A startling piercing scream—in a melodious feminine voice—comes through the Opening]

Private O'Flynn. [Suddenly dropping his Musket, he assumes a gesture of Horror]

Lieut. Blossom. [From his elevated berth, he tumbles head foremost, out on the Stage, and utters a groan of distress]

Blanche. [In Gray Mantilla and Tricolor Cap, her beautiful long Hair in a Plait falling down over her back—deathly pale, franticly emerging from Right Rear, and running in past the Guard—suddenly halting, and looking indignantly fro n the Officer to the Guard and back—in caustic rebuking tone] You cowardly fellows!—You tried to shoot me down!—[Looking eagerly around—in commanding tone] Lead me to Captain Daponte!—

Lieut. Blossom. [Assuming a pompous bearing—in tone of condescension] The Colonel is not in the Camp, at present—

Blanche. [She looks hopefully at the Guard]

Private O'Flynn. [Bowing submissively to her—in respectful tone] The Colonel is away, lady—and all of his Command that he didn't carry with him, is now before you—

Blanche. [With a gesture of mortification looking at them— in tone of chagrin] Captain Daponte is my dear Brother!—and it was to meet him that I have come from Belair!—

Lieut. Blossom. [Facing her, and looking critically at her— in incisive tone] How were you able to get through the Yankee lines—

Blanche. [Looking disdainfully at him—in contemptuous tone] It is not my pleasure to tell you, Sir!—

Lieut. Blossom. [Looking determinedly at her—in tone of high authority] Until the Colonel returns—when I will take you before him, to account for yourself—you will be detained in this Camp.—

Private O'Flynn. [Leveling at her, his Musket] Halt!—

Blanche. [In tone of anxiety—Aside] Colonel Ferguson is in danger of Capture at Belair!—[Looking contemptuously at Blossom—in tone of defiance] Dare you hold me Prisoner in my Brother's Camp!—

Lieut. Blossom. [Looking derisively at her—in scoffing tone] In this Camp—until Daponte returns—

Private O'Flynn. [Leveling at her, his Musket] Halt!—

Blanche. [With a gesture of Horror backing, a step—in a tone of abhorrence] With *brutes* for my only Companions!—

Private O'Flynn. [With a gesture of alarm he bounds up to Right Rear and assumes a listening attitude.—Immediately dropping his Musket, and bounding toward Right Front—in tone of consternation] The "BLUE COATS!"—

Lieut. Blossom. [Bounding after him—in imploring tone] Guard!—don't leave me!—

Blanche. [Anxiously looking around—in tone of despair] What can I do to save myself!—[She runs into Tent]

Major Perkins. [Through Middle Rear, with Sword drawn, he stealthily bounds in, with a Squad of "Blue Coats"]

Lieut. N. B. Rhinelander. [A German Federal Officer. Of robust frame, and above the average height. About 35.—Through Right Rear, with Sword drawn, he noiselessly bounds in, with a Squad of "Blue Coats"]

Major Perkins. [Halting—in savage tone] What do we find!— [Looking around—in tone of disappointment] An abandoned Camp!—[Looking into Tent—in demoniac tone of triumph] Aha!—playing "hide—and—seek."—I thought I would, some day, get a chance to put a "Rope" around your White Neck!—

Blanche. [With a bearing of Resignation, she emerges from the Tent]

Major Perkins. [Turning round, pointing back] Lieutenant! put a Guard at once on her!—and if she's disposed to be troublesome, load her down in Irons!—[Pointing to rear of Tent] And see if there is not another one—for Vipers always go in Pairs.—'

Blanche. [With a gesture of Horror—in despairing tone—Aside] My God!—he means to kill me!—and I am helpless!

Silas Doubleday. [A Blue Coat Scout, well above the average height—bounding in, Right Rear, and pointing exult·ingly back] A Squad of "Rebs" coming from Belair, with a "Blue Coat" Prisoner.—

Major Perkins. [In tone of Command] Ambuscade, my Men!—[In exultant tone] and we'll "bag" them!—

Silas Doubleday. [He bounds back out Right Rear]

Major Perkins. [He stations himself and his Men, to Front of Entrance—well out of sight from Outside]

Lieut. Rhinelander. [He stations himself and his Men, to Rear of Entrance—well out of sight from Outside]

    [The tread of Troops approaching at a rapid pace, shouting and hurrahing, comes from Off, Right Rear]

Blanche. [She is noticed stealthily edging toward Right Front—suddenly throwing up her arms, in an attitude of thankfulness to Heaven, she noiselessly bounds out of sight]

Lieut. Allen Pillow. [A young Confederate Officer of lithe muscular frame—a little above the average height.—With his discomfited Prisoner and his jubilant Command, he bounds in sight]

Major Perkins.   }
Lieut. Rhinelander. } [With their Men bounding forward—in determined tone] Throw down your Arms!—and Surrender!—

Lieut. Pillow. [Promptly complying—in ironical tone] You have the "Drop" on us, Major—ha! ha!

Major Perkins. [In tone of peremptory command] Lieutenant! take their arms from the Traitors!—and put a Guard on them—until we are leaving—

Lieut. Rhinelander. [He joyfully seizes Colonel Ferguson by the hand]

Colonel Ferguson. [Joyfully seizing him by the hand] How can I thank you, Major Perkins!—

Major Perkins. [Looking cynically at him—in tone of dissatisfaction] After my warning to you about "BELAIR," [Pointing back across] how did you let her to pass through your Lines—[Looking across—with a gesture of Horror—in tone of mortification] Has the Traitress escaped from me!—[Pointing to Right Front] Lieutenant Rhinelander!—Go—bring her back!—if it takes my whole Command!—

Silas Doubleday. [Bounding in Right Rear—promptly pointing back—in tone of warning] Daponte's returning, Major—on the "Double Quick"—

Major Perkins. [Promptly looking across at him] Lieutenant Rhinelander!—[Motioning him to Left Rear] "FORWARD" is the word.—

Lieutenant Rhinelander. [With hasty step, he starts toward Left Rear]

Colonel Ferguson. [Seriously looking at the Major—in tone of anxiety] I hope Colonel Daponte's sudden attack was not a *Ruse*—that draws Captain O'Harra—with the small force at his command—away from the defence of the "Fort!"—

Silas Doubleday. [In assuring tone] The "Johnnies" are bringing in no Prisoners—and they got the worst of the "Fight."—[He bounds back, and out]

Major Perkins. [Looking composedly at him—in assuring tone] Ned O'Harra is as wiley as he is brave, and if Daponte was trying to fool him, he has been beaten at his own Game.—

Lieut. Rhinelander. [In Teutonic loud tone] *Forward*—MARCH.—[Quickly turning round, he leads through the Opening]

Major Perkins.)
Colonel Ferguson. } [Close behind, they promptly depart, together]

Colonel Ferguson. [Suddenly turning round, at Opening, and looking vengefully across the Quarters—in tone of mortification] They have my Horse!—[In sympathetic tone] And I'm sorry for APPOMATTOX!—[In rebuking tone] for they'll *starve* the poor brute!—and *ride him to death!* [Quickly turning away, he hastily departs]

[Immediately, a Horse is heard restlessly pawing the Ground, outside Middle Right, and violently kicking the strong plank wall. Immediately, a Horse is heard viciously kicking the wall, a little to Front. Suddenly, a Crash is heard—and high up in the wall, too large Open Windows show—through which two Horses—presumably confined in adjacent Stalls—promptly protrude their Heads. On the Head of the Rear Horse, a Starry Banner is conspicuously displayed. On that of the other, the Confederate Flag is equally conspicuous.—After a furious little "Battle of Flags"—in which each tries without success to capture the "Color" of the other— they withdraw their Heads. And judging by their kicking of walls, they are trying to break out of their Stalls, to get into closer engagement.—Immediately, they are heard violently Rearing—with the scene of their combat shifting in a Right Rear direction. Suddenly, "APPOMATTOX"—with "Color" flying—dashes past Middle Rear—presumably following his "Blue Coat" Master—"ANDREW JACKSON"—minus his "Flag"—bedaubed with Mud, and with Hair bristled—in high dudgeon in hot pursuit]

[Immediately, the noise of the entry of Troops—with the Clanking of Arms—comes through Middle Rear.]

Lieut. Burke Davis. [A young Confederate Officer. Of well-developed muscular frame—well above the average height—in greatly disarranged Uniform, and looking very pale—with slow step entering through Middle Rear—looking considerately around back—in sympathetic tone] I hope it is not that bad, Miss Daponte—

Blanche. [Entering beside him—suddenly bounding before him, and with a gesture of Horror looking at him—in thrilling tone of alarm] You "hope!"—is that all!— [In heart-rending tone] And I can only "hope!"— [With clasped hands pressing her heart—looking earnestly at him—in tone of resignation] Now, I want to know the worst!—

Lieut. Davis. [In serious tone] We couldn't stand the impetuous Charge of the Savages let loose upon us—who consisted in great part of infuriated Indians and Wild Irishmen!—And in single combat with him, our Colonel was carried off, Prisoner, by a red-faced Warrior.— And the worst, I hope, is that he is now on his way to a Yankee Prison—where he will be held until duly "Exchanged."—

Blanche. [In tone of startling earnestness] My Brother must not lie pining—perhaps dying!—in a loathsome Prison, while I have my liberty!—And I want to be immediately escorted beyond your lines—in the direction of the Fort to which he was taken!—

Lieut Davis. [In deferential tone] You shall be escorted as you wish, Miss Daponte.—[Promptly starting toward Middle Rear—turning round] But you will be made Prisoner when you get to the Yankee Outpost—[In scoffing tone] in your foolhardy and idle undertaking.

Blanche. [Looking rebukingly after him—in emphatic tone] When a true woman works with a will for the man she loves, there is no telling her ingenuity to foil his enemies!—[Looking deferentially at audience] And if a little Mouse was strong enough—as we are informed— to set at liberty an imprisoned Lion, [Pointing deliberately to herself] a spirited Creole Girl—with her hot Southern blood coursing [Holding up her arms] the bluest of "Blue" veins—should be strong enough to tear down the Bars behind which lies—perhaps bleeding and unattended—a Brother whom she loves!—loves with a devoted Sister's love!—[Starting Rear—turning back—in declaratory tone] I am not of that round num-

ber of faint-hearted Girls who take their courage from
their fears. And on my mission of love I go—[Majes-
tically turning away—rapidly departing—quickly turning round at Door—in startling tone of earnestness] TO
DO OR DIE!

[End of Scene I.

SCENE II. [A "HALT on the Route of the "Blue Coats" returning to "Fort Union"—after their victorious "fight" with
Colonel Daponte and his Men. A little Left of Middle—
against Rear—a rude temporary seat shows. Right
and Left, wide open Entrances show]

Captain O'Harra. [Approaching, Left—in triumphant jocular
tone] We've got the "Johnnies" again, this time.—
[Bounding in, his Uniform torn, and in a laughably
disarranged condition—above his head swinging his
Sword—in exultant tone] A "Roland" for an "Oliver"—
tit for tat is the Latin of it, I believe.—If they have Ferguson, [Turning round and pointing back] we have
Daponte—ha! ha!—

Colonel Daponte. [In greatly torn Uniform—Guarded by
two "Blue Coat" Soldiers—with head bowed he enters]

Captain O'Harra. [Thrusting his hand into an inside Breast
Pocket—in Commanding tone] Halt for "Refresh-
ment"—

Colonel Daponte. [He bounds into the near Seat]

Captain O Harra. [Drawing forth a huge Flask, and shaking
it—in tone of mock gravity] The Priest Christens his
own child, first—ha! ha!—[Throwing wide apart, his
legs, and raising his Flask, and taking a generous
draught, and going up to his Prisoner, and looking considerately down at him, and offering him his Flask—in
cordial tone] Take a little, Colonel—of the Staff of life—
ha! ha!—'Tis a long way to the "Fort"—and 'twill brace
you up—

Colonel Daponte. [Shaking his bowed head—in thankful tone]
I never "Drink," Captain—

[His Guards look astonished at each other]

Captain O'Harra. [Backing, a step, and looking rebukingly down at him] You won't "Drink" with me!—and you want to insult me!—

Colonel Daponte. [Looking earnestly up at him] I repeat, Captain O'Harra, that I never "Drink"—and if any of my Men do, it is against my positive "Orders."—[He bows down his head]

[With eyes wide open—showing their "whites"—his Guards look Front]

Captain O'Harra. [With a gesture of astonishment—in serious tone—Aside] That's the whole story in a nutshell— why his splendid Command didn't scoop up myself and my little band of Heroes.—[Exultingly holding up his Flask—Aside] It didn't have the right kind of "Ammunition"—ha! ha!—[Looking seriously down at him—in tone of astonishment] You never get "Drunk," Colonel!—Then, you know nothing of one of the chief enjoyments of this life!—

Colonel Daponte. [Looking composedly up at him—in emphatic tone] "Water"—pure "Water" has been my favorite beverage, up to this time—and I don't know what a "headache" is.—[Suddenly relapsing into his lassitude, he bows down his head]

Captain O'Harra. [Looking critically down at him—in serious inquiring tone] Don't take a "Nightcap," before going to Bed—nor a "Toddy" every morning before Breakfast—in this Climate—

[His Guards are noticed smacking their lips]

Colonel Daponte. [Looking guilelessly up at him—gravely shaking his head—in languid tone] Don't know what you mean, Captain—

[With eyes wide open—showing their "Whites"—his Guards look Front, again]

Captain O'Harra. [Gravely looking down at him—in inquiring confident tone] Surely, your "Prison Fare"—especially for high Officers—includes "Whiskey"—for an "Appetizer"—

Colonel Daponte. [Looking candidly up at him] I never keep
in my Camp—for any purpose—a drop of the vile
Stuff!—And if any of my Prisoners want an "Appetizer,"
they must do without it!—or take my "Appetizer"—
"Water"—pure "Water."—
　　　　[His Guards look shocked]

Captain O'Harra. [Looking furiously at him—in sarcastic
rebuking tone] No "Whiskey" in your "Prison Fare"
for "Officers!"—[Vigorously stamping the ground—in
emphatic determined tone] Then, I want Colonel
Ferguson released—without delay—from your infernal
Prison Pen!—[He petulantly turns away]

Colonel Daponte. [Bounding to his feet, and eagerly approaching the Captain, a step—in tone of astonishment]
Colonel Ferguson!—

Captain O'Harra. [Turning half round and coolly looking
back—in blunt tone] Colonel Ferguson—who, two weeks
ago, relieved Major Perkins. He was captured, to-day,
at Belair, by your Men—

Colonel Daponte. [In eager inquiring tone] "Gus" Ferguson—

Captain O'Harra. [Promptly facing him—in frank tone]
Colonel "Gus" Ferguson—of the "Oldham Blues."—[In
tone of defiance] And may be you have some old grudge
against the gallant Northerner—

Colonel Daponte. [With a gesture of rapture] "Gus" Ferguson
was the dearest friend I had living, when I was at
Stafford College!—

Captain O'Harra. [Pointing through Left Entrance] He's a
Prisoner at your Camp.—[Approaching him, a step]
He's an excellent fellow.—And if he is of Puritan
Stock, he has no more use for "Cold Water"—as an
"Appetizer"—than I have.—And if you promise me to
set him at liberty, immediately—

Colonel Daponte. [Pointing impressively to his heart] I give
you my "Word of honor," Captain—

Captain O'Harra. [In blunt tone] That's enough, Colonel—
[Assuming a military bearing—in emphatic tone]
always enough, between *Soldiers.*—

Colonel Daponte. [Joyfully taking hold of his hand—in ardent tone] Captain! our next meeting, I hope, [Looking significantly at him] will be a merry one.—[With a smiling face he bows away toward Left Entrance]

Captain O'Harra. [Holding up his Flask] But you are leaving without making your peace with me—ha! ha!—

Colonel Daponte. [Bounding up to him, he eagerly seizes the offered Flask, and throwing back his head—in veteran Drinker fashion—raises it to his lips]
[His late Guards look astonished at each other]

Captain O'Harra. [His impatience to get back his Flask, soon manifests itself, in his restlessness]

Colonel Daponte. [Panting for breath, handing back Flask—in tone of satisfaction] Captain! I never needed it more.—[Suddenly turning away, looking back—in tone of mock seriousness] But I never "Drink"—[With bounding step departing—in hearty tone] ha! ha!! ha!!!

Captain O'Harra. [Shaking his Flask, he petulantly throws it on the ground. Drawing forth another one, and exultingly holding it up] The true "Captain" will always have his "Reserves" to fall back upon—in case of necessity—ha! ha!—[Taking a satisfactory draught—glancing back over his shoulder—shaking Flask—in confident serious tone—Aside] If they get it into their hands, good by to it.—[Turning round, and assuming a pompous bearing—in commanding tone] Squad—ATTENTION. Right—FACE. Forward—MARCH.

[The "Guards" depart by Right Entrance]
[Promptly following Guards—suddenly halting at Right Entrance—in thunder tone] Squad—HALT.—[Pointing admiringly after his command, looking around at audience—in earnest tone] The Nation's brave Defenders to-day, will never die!—[Advancing Front—in confident tone] In every foreign land, they will live in the admiration of the Friends of human Liberty; and in Story and in Song, they will be enshrined in their own dear land!—[Raising his Flask, and "Drinking"—in tone of felicitation] The Country

is Safe!—[Looking significantly back at Right Entrance—in positive tone] And it shall be the highest
duty of her Loyal Statesmen, to provide generously
for the gallant and patriotic maimed Survivors, and to
take good care of the Widows and the Orphans of the
fallen heroes!—[In humorous tone—Aside] They could
easily take care of mine—ha! ha!—[Taking a "Drink,"
and exultingly holding up his Flask—in maudlin humorous tone] I'll fight it out on this Line—while my "Ammunition" lasts—ha! ha!—[Going up to temporary
Seat, and falling heavily on it, and setting his Flask on
the ground beside him, and with a smiling face looking
at audience—in maudlin jovial tone] "Holding the
Fort"—ha! ha!—[Picking up Flask, and "Drinking"—
suddenly taking it down and significantly shaking it—
petulantly throwing it on the ground—in maudlin tone
of disappointment] I'm out of "AMMUNITION!"—and
must now break up Camp.—[Struggling to his feet,
and with unsteady step starting toward Right Entrance—in maudlin exultant tone] "DIVIDED"—
[Staggering] we *stand.*—No—that isn't it.—[Steadying
himself] "UNITED"—[Staggering] we *fall.*—[Steady-
ing himself] No—no—[Reeling through Right Entrance—in maudlin triumphant tone] WE'LL NEVER
FALL!

[End of Scene II.]

SCENE III. [Scene I, repeated]

[The Band is playing a mournful air]

Lieut. Burke Davis. [Left—a little to Front of Tent—he
stands reading from the Muster-Roll in his hand]

Lieut. Blossom. [At a short distance across, he stands
listening]

Private O'Flynn. [To Right—a little Front of Blossom—he
stands with mouth wide open, and eyes agape, listening]

[A Private Soldier, with White Bandage on his head,
stands at Middle Rear, languidly looking in]

Colonel Daponte. [With head bowed, he is excitedly pacing to and fro—from Right to Left—across the Stage, at a short distance to Front]

Lieut. Burke Davis. [Laying down Roll, and looking across at the Colonel—in serious tone] And Corporal Maloney is "Missing"—

Private O'Flynn. [Impressively pointing his finger at the Lieutenant—in sorrowful confident tone] You can put poor Mullowny down with your "Killed," Leftenant— for "Patsy" liked "foighting" like "ating," and it was on the loikes of him that the "Blue Coats" began their *"killing in earnest'* our "Boys "

Colonel Daponte. [In soliloquy—in tone of humiliation] A little Troop of Federal Raiders boldly *ambuscade* in my Camp—and capture my Men as they triumphantly enter with their Prisoner!—

Private O'Flynn. [In serious tone—Aside] They very near got Blossom and me, too.—

Colonel Daponte. [In despairing tone] What hope is there for us, to wrest victory from an enemy of unsurpassed daring, vigilance, and valor, and of unlimited resources!— [In confident tone] The Fates are against us!—[In self-accusing tone] Heaven is against us!

Private O'Flynn. [Hanging his head—Aside] Then, the game is up with us!—whin they're agin us *up there.* [He puts his hand to his throat, and feels it tenderly]

Colonel Daponte. [Halting, and dejectedly facing audience— in despairing tone] We have enlisted our last man capable of bearing arms. And our lines of communication with our chief Sources of Supply, are closed by a Blockade that deprives us of all intercourse with the outer world!—And if among foreign Nations, we have a friend to-day, in our *life-struggle,* it is England—[He contemplatively hangs his head]

Private O'Flynn. [In malicious tone—Aside] Bad luck to her!—it was her support—that wasn't for love of us— that put solid agin us, the brave Irish "Boys," with their "GREEN FLAGS!—"

Colonel Daponte. [Abstractedly repeating it] England—[In petulant tone] whose open countenance induced us to overrate our Strength, and to reject advantageous overtures for Peace!—

Blanche. [Bounding in, Right Rear—in rapturous tone] He said my Brother was "Exchanged!"—and would be here before me!—[Suddenly halting, she looks eagerly through the Quarters]

Colonel Daponte. [With a gesture of surprise looking at the audience—in tone of astonishment] Blanche's Voice!—[With a gesture of Horror—in tone of anxiety] Does it come from the Other World!—

Blanche. [In eager distressful tone] *Where* is he!—

Colonel Daponte. [He joyfully turns round]

Blanche. [Bounding toward him—in tone of rapture] My Brother!—

Colonel Daponte. [Impulsively advancing to meet her—in ardent tone] My Sister!—

Blanche. [Impressing upon his cheek, an ardent kiss, and through her tears of joy looking up at him—in tone of satisfaction] They told me that you were captured in Battle!—and I started to the Yankee Fort—to liberate you, or die in the attempt!—

Colonel Daponte. [Affectionately seizing both her hands—in tone of alarm] My Sister! you are not looking well!—

Private O'Flynn. [He bounds into Tent]

Colonel Daponte. Your eyes have lost much of their lustre—and the Rose has left your cheek!—You tremble!—and I fear you are ill!—

Private O'Flynn. [He bounds out of Tent with a Camp Stool, and sets it for her]

Colonel Daponte. [He promptly bows his thanks to the gallant Private]

Private O'Flynn. [Glancing reflectingly at Burke Davis and Blossom—in exultant tone—Aside] It takes an Irishman to show proper respect to a Lady—

[Suddenly, a startling Outburst of Cheers—immediately followed by a volley of terrifying Yells—comes through Middle Rear]

Lieut. Burke Davis.
Lieut. Blossom.
Private O'Flynn. [With bounding step, they depart through Middle Rear]

Colonel Daponte. [Turning to Blanche—in inspiring tone] Don't be alarmed, my Sister—[With hasty step he departs through Middle Rear]

Blanche. [With a gesture of Horror facing the audience—solemnly raising her hands, and looking reverently upward—in earnest tone of supplication] Oh! that it were the will of All-powerful Heaven, to restore to our distracted Country the Peace that made her the Elysium of Nations!—to stop this Sacrilegious "War!"—this Murderous Conflict!—that is filling our delightful and surpassingly fertile land, with the desolate Homes of weeping Widows and fatherless Orphans!—and whose *most enduring Monument*—[Pointing solemnly ahead down to the ground] the *gloomy Vaults* shall be, which shall hold the bones of *dead Heroes!—dead Brothers!*—[With a gesture of Horror] BROTHERS SLAIN!—[Stamping the ground—in startling tone of condemnation] SLAIN BY BROTHERS!

Colonel Daponte. [He hastily enters through Middle Rear, and heads toward Middle Right, eagerly perusing a lengthy paper in his hand]

Confederate Courier. [A Red-Haired, beardless Confederate Soldier—under average height—of angular, muscular frame, in Boots and Spurs—he bounds in beside the Colonel]

Lieut Burke Davis.
Lieut. Blossom. [Immediately behind they bound in, together, and head, Left—toward Front of Tent]

Private O'Flynn. [A number of Confederate Privates clamorously bound in at the heels of the Officers—Private O'Flynn leading, on their left—looking around at them——in assuring tone] *A "GINERAL ORDHER!"*—

[A Confederate Private, with bandaged head, limps to Door, and looks languidly in]

[Burke Davis, Blossom, Private O'Flynn, and the other Privates, quickly form into a circular line—from Front to Rear—before the Colonel and the Courier]

Colonel Daponte. [Looking across at his men, and holding up his document—in tone of gratification] You are highly complimented, in "General Orders"—

Private O'Flynn. [The Privates] Hurrah!—Hurrah!—Hurrah!

Colonel Daponte. For your Patriotism—your Patience—and your Bravery—

Private O'Flynn. [The Privates—in exultant tone] We have "whipped" the "Mudsills," everywhere!—Hurrah!—Hurrah!

Colonel Daponte. [Laying down his document and looking ruefully at them—in serious tone] Our gallant Army is dwindling away fast—[Illustratively holding up his document—and falling back, a step—in serious assuring tone] and we are now fighting on the "Defensive!"—[With a gesture of Horror—illustratively pointing around, falling back—in startling tone of alarm] *And the enemy in force is closing around us!*

Private O'Flynn. [With gestures of astonishment, the Privates hear the startling disclosure]

Colonel Daponte. [Looking despairingly at his men—in grave assuring tone] And the dear *"Cause"* [Glancing confidently around at his Sister—in emphatic tone] to which all of us would give our lives—

Private O'Flynn. [The Privates—in thrilling Martyr tone] We would!—we would!—

Colonel Daponte. [Holding up his document, and demonstratively shaking it—in tremulous despairing tone] Is now a "LOST CAUSE!"—[He suddenly bows down his head]

Blanche. [From her place near Centre Front—in startling determined tone] NO!—[Heroically bounding before the Soldiers, and looking inspiringly at them—in startling emphatic tone] NO!—[Vehemently stamping the ground] A "JUST CAUSE" is never "*lost!*"—

Private O'Flynn. [The Privates—looking admiringly at her—in rapturous tone of applause] Bravo!—Bravo!—A JOAN!—[Yelling to Right Front and to Left Front] NO!—NO!—

Private O'Flynn. [With a gesture of surprise—in tone of exultation—Aside] A Second "Maid of Orleans!"—

Bud Talbot. [Bounding in through Left Front—in startling tone of alarm] The "Blue Coats" are coming in force!—[Bounding toward the Colonel—in earnest tone] Lieutenant Pillow and his Men have "Escaped!"—[Pointing to Right Front] They are coming this way!—with Major Perkins with his whole Command in hot pursuit!—[He bounds out through Right Front]

Private O'Flynn. [Looking inspiringly at his Comrades—in a thrilling Exclamation] Our Guns!—[Bounding toward Middle Rear] Our Guns!

Private O'Flynn. [The Other Privates bound after Private O'Flynn—Yelling] Our Guns!—Our Guns!—

Colonel Daponte. [Drawing his sword, he promptly takes position, near Right Front]

Confed Courier. [Drawing his sword, he bounds to position, at Centre Front]

Lieut. Burke Davis. [Drawing his sword, he aligns himself in position, Left, near Front]

Lieut. Blossom. [Turning right round, he bounds into Tent]

Blanche. [Bounding furiously after him—in sarcastic tone of rebuke] Craven!—[With a firm back hold on his Coat Collar, immediately emerging from the Tent with Blossom, and throwing him Front—in indignant tone] Did you want to show the "White Feather!"—and bring disgrace on the "Gray!"—

Colonel Daponte. [He bounds up to Blanche, and taking firm hold of her arm, and starting with her toward Right Rear—in tone of solicitude] You will be safe here, my Sister—and out of our way—

[Suddenly, the auditory hear the Clashing of Swords, the blows of "Clubbed" Muskets, and the loud imprecations of bloodthirsty combatants, at a near point, Off, Right Front]

Colonel Daponte. [Suddenly turning round, he bounds toward position, Right Front]

Bud Talbot. [Bounding in through Right Front—pointing back—in tone of satisfaction] Lieut. Pillow and his Men!—[He bounds out through Left Front]

Major Perkins. [In bloodthirsty tone] Take them back— *dead or alive!—*

Lieut. Pillow. [Warding off the heavy blows dealt at him by his pursuer, he backs into sight]
[With their "Clubbed" Muskets defending themselves, the "Grays" back hastily into sight, before the "Blue Coats"]

Blanche. [From Right Rear, she bounds in on the Stage, and looking Front, assumes the bearing of a Heroine]

Lieut. Pillow. [His Sword is immediately stricken from his Grasp]

Major Perkins. [In bloodthirsty tone] We give no Quarter!—

Colonel Daponte. [With Sword raised, he bounds in the way of the savage "Blue Coat" Officer]

Bud Talbot. [*Hors de combat*, he backs hastily in through Left Front]

Lieut. Rhinelander. [With Sword raised, he enters in close pursuit]

Silas Doubleday. [He bounds in beside him]
[A number of "Blue Coats" bound in at the heels of the Officers]

Lieut. Rhinelander. [In German accent—in bloodthirsty tone] We take no "Brisners!"—

Lieut. Burke Davis. [With Sword raised, he bounds in the way of the bloodthirsty Rhinelander]

Silas Doubleday. [Drawing his Sword, he charges upon the Confederate Courier]

[Before the augmented force of "Blue Coats," the "Grays" back precipitantly to Rear]

Lieut Blossom. [He bounds behind Burke Davis]

The "Blues." [They are fast putting the "Grays," *Hors de combat*]

Blanche. [Heroically bounding before the "Grays"—in startling rallying tone] Are you Southern Men!—

The "Grays." [With a terrible "Yell," they desperately charge upon the victorious "Blue Coats," and press them back]

Blanche. [She picks up a Musket dropped by a Blue Coat, and fires it at a stalworth "Blue Coat's head]

Lieut. Blossom. [Groaning, he falls to the ground]

Blanche. ["Clubbing" her Musket, she bounds to the assistance of the "Grays"]

Private O'Flynn. [He bounds in through Middle Rear, and "Clubbing" his Musket, leaps with a terrible Yell into the midst of the "Blue Coats"—and striking right and left, brings down one with every blow]

Colonel Daponte. [He is noticed fighting desperately on the defensive]

Lieut. Burke Davis. [He is precipitantly backing from his savage antagonist]

Major Perkins. [In bloodthirsty tone] We give no "Quarter!"—

Blanche. [Throwing down her Musket, she bounds for another one—lying on the ground]

Lieut. Rhinelander. [In bloodthirsty tone] We take no "Brisners!"—

Silas Doubleday. }
Confederate Courier. } [They clinch, and both go down—and rolling on the ground, they are noticed fighting furiously]

Colonel Daponte. [He falls on one Knee]

Blanche. [With a bound she stands beside her Brother, with her Musket determinedly aimed at his savage antagonist's head]

Major Perkins. [He promptly drops his arms to his sides]

Blanche [In startling determined tone] We give no "Quarter!"—

Lieut. Rhinelander. [With Sword raised, he savagely starts to the relief of his superior Officer]

Private O'Flynn. [Bounding to cross the murderous "Blue Coat" Officer—in startling tone of determination] No!—You don't!—[In an instant he is in Rhinelander's way, and has him looking into the Muzzle of his formidable Musket]

Lieut. Rhinelander. [Trembling, and looking aghast, he drops his arms to his sides]

Private O'Flynn. [Looking determinedly at him—in retorting tone] We take no Prisoners!—

Confederate Courier. [Planting his heel on the chest of his antagonist—stretched on the ground, *Hors de combat*—and straightening himself to his full height, he triumphantly waves aloft his Sword]

[A startling shout of triumph comes from the "Grays," at Rear]

[Immediately, with awe-inspiring solemnity, A LARGE WHITE BANNER shows slowly entering at Left Rear, and extending across the Stage—showing inscribed on it, as it develops, unintelligible Large Black Letters]

[The "fighting is immediately suspended, and with gestures of Solicitude, the combatants look Rear]

[Suddenly a Clattering—as that of a Horseman approaching at a high rate of speed—comes from Off, Left Rear]

[As the Clattering comes from a nearer point, incessant loud Cheering comes from Off, Left Rear]

[Immediately, the rapid firing of Cannon comes from Off, Left Rear—and will continue to the Fall of the Curtain]

[Immediately, a "Blue Coat" Courier dashes past, with a Coal Black Steed carrying waving above his

head, a Starry Banner—immediately followed by a mob
of "Blue Coats," shouting joyfully; and the White Banner—extending across the Stage—shows inscribed on it,
the mysterious word A P P O M A T T O X]

[Immediately, the Confederate Flag descends rapidly,
from its high place on the Flagstaff; and the "Stars and
Stripes" ascends on the opposite side]

[The Confederates promptly throw down their arms,
and with heads bowed Start Front]

[With heads erect, the Blue Coats form into Line
across the Stage—at Middle—facing Rear, and exultingly looking at their victorious Flag]

[The Confederates quickly form into Line across the
Stage—facing Front, with heads bowed]

[The Confederate Flag descends out of sight, and the
"Stars and Stripes" waves at the top of the Flagstaff]

[Immediately the Band plays the "Star Spangled
Banner"]

[The Confederates quickly turn round, and bow to
the "Old Flag"]

[The Blue Coats promptly turn round, and bounding
Front, cordially take by the hand, their gallant and
patriotic late antagonists]

[Bounding Front, and withdrawing from her bosom,
a glittering Starry Banner, and rapturously looking at
the audience, Blanche patriotically waves aloft, the Old
Flag that she had never ceased to admire]

[Tableau.]

[End of Scene III.]

[END OF ACT V.]